A.W.A.R.E.
Our World, Our Water

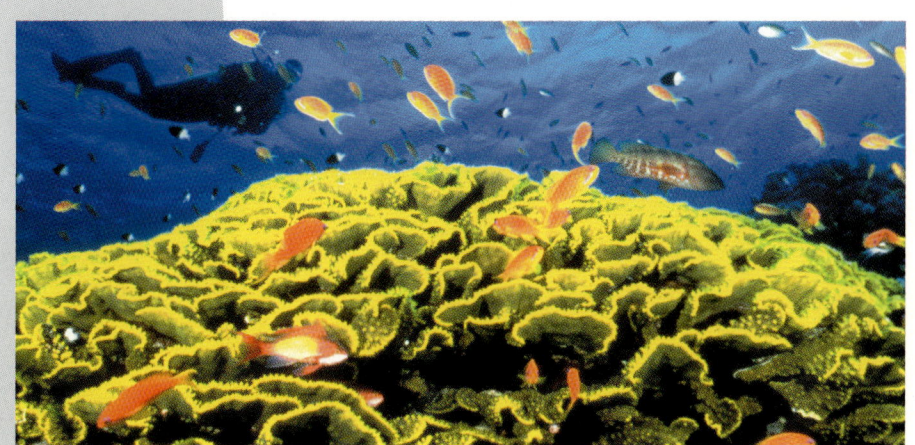

PROJECT AWARE MANUAL

© International PADI, Inc. 2000
All rights reserved.

No part of this book may be reproduced in any form without written permission of the publisher.

Produced by Divng Science and Technology
for International PADI, Inc.

Published and distributed by
PADI
30151 Tomas Street
Rancho Santa Margarita, CA 92688-2125

Library of Congress Card Number 2001131139
ISBN 1-878663-26-7

Printed in the United States of America
10 9 8 7 6 5 4 3 2 1

Product No. 70241 (11/00) Version 1

ACKNOWLEDGEMENTS

Editor in Chief
Drew Richardson

Development, Instructional Design, Consultation and Review
Lori Bachelor-Smith
Pat Fousek
Mary Kaye Nesbit
John Kinsella
Tiffany Leite
Jeff Myers
Drew Richardson
Karl Shreeves
Brad Smith
Susan Tate
Kristin Valette
Bob Wohlers

International Review and Consultation
Kurt Amsler
Juerg Beeli
Jan Moeller Busch
Yosihiro Inoue
Jean-Claude Monachon
Henrik Nimb
Olle Olsson
Suzanne Pleydell

Technical Writing
Lori Bachelor-Smith
Alex Brylske
Todd R. Menzel

Editing
Lori Bachelor-Smith
Todd R. Menzel
Susan E. Tate

Layout and Design
Carol Porter
Dail Schroeder

Illustrations
Greg Beatty

Photography
Kurt Amsler
Jack Archibald
Peter Auster, National Undersea Research Center (NURC)
Robert Baker
Ken Berry
Alex Brylske
Center for Marine Conservation
Peter Dreisel
Claire Ellis
Anthony Ellis
Ecoscene
Bret Forbes
Douglas Good
Tom Haight
Carol Haney
Brigit Jager
Bill Jurney
Mary Kaye Nesbit
Bob Leite
Tiffany Leite
Michigan Sea Grant
Amos Nachoum
John Nesbit
National Oceanic and Atmospheric Administration (NOAA)
Alese Pechter
Mort Pechter
Doug Perrine, Innerspace Visions
Philip Pinto
Jeremy Stafford-Deitsch
Kristin Valette
Michel Verdure
Bob Wholers
Reef Relief
R.E.E.F.

Cover Photography
Cliff Wassmann
Robert Zimmerman
Michel Verdure
Kevin Wilton

© Michel Verdure

TABLE OF CONTENTS

CHAPTER ONE
INTRODUCTION
Introduction 4
How to Use This Book 7
Project AWARE 8

CHAPTER TWO
THE AQUATIC WORLD
Earth's Aquatic Environment 16
Freshwater Ecosystems 21
The Ocean and Seas 25
Marine Productivity 26
The Coastal Zone 31

CHAPTER THREE
TEMPERATE AND POLAR WATERS
Ocean Productivity 39
Life Between the Tides...............41
Kelp Forests...............49
Polar Regions...............54

CHAPTER FOUR
CORAL REEFS
Coral Reefs – Diversity and Beauty 62
Reef Fish 67
Limits of Abundance 71
Threats – Natural and Human-induced 72

CHAPTER FIVE
AQUATIC RESOURCES IN PERIL
Pollution 80
Fisheries Concerns...................91
Coastal Zone and Wetland Degradation 101

CHAPTER SIX
TROUBLED WATERS
The World's Most Environmentally Threatened Regions...............106

CHAPTER SEVEN
CURRENT STATUS AND FUTURE SOLUTIONS
Fisheries – Responsible Management 121
Coastal Zone Management...................128
International Measures 130

CHAPTER EIGHT
WHAT YOU CAN DO TO PROTECT THE AQUATIC ENVIRONMENT
Diving Aware 134
Getting Involved 137
Removing Debris From the Aquatic Environment 138
Mooring Buoys...............141
Marine Protected Areas 142
Artificial Reefs 144
The Future...............148

GLOSSARY
REFERENCES
INDEX
KNOWLEDGE REVIEW

CHAPTER ONE
INTRODUCTION

INTRODUCTION

"How odd it seems that we call our home planet Earth when it is so clearly Ocean."

– Arthur C. Clark

Water is life. All of us – every living creature – depend upon the earth's ocean, seas, rivers, streams and lakes, not only for water, but for food, transportation, power, health and recreation. As human beings, our relationship with the water surrounding us is complex. We find beauty and wonder in the creatures that live in and around aquatic environments, and often find solace in just gazing out over the water's surface. Yet, at the same time, we seek to control water resources and exploit them for our benefit. Our connection to the water world is both undeniable and critical, now and in the future.

As we enter a new millennium, an inescapable fact of global life is that our aquatic environment is in trouble. While it's true that there are some success stories – a few freshwater environments are in better shape today than they were 25 years ago – no such claim can be made about the ocean. However, environmental advocates are working hard every day to make this better. In the last several decades we have seen an increase in awareness and education about the problems facing our oceans that has led to many effective movements to better the aquatic environment.

"We want to feel that our children, their children and generations to come will be able to enjoy the underwater world that has given us so much. There are many significant problems facing mankind, but this is truly our cause. If divers do not take an active role in preserving the aquatic realm, who will?"

– John J. Cronin, CEO, PADI

INTRODUCTION

- **INTRODUCTION**
- **HOW TO USE THIS BOOK**
- **PROJECT AWARE**

Photo by NOAA/Department of Commerce

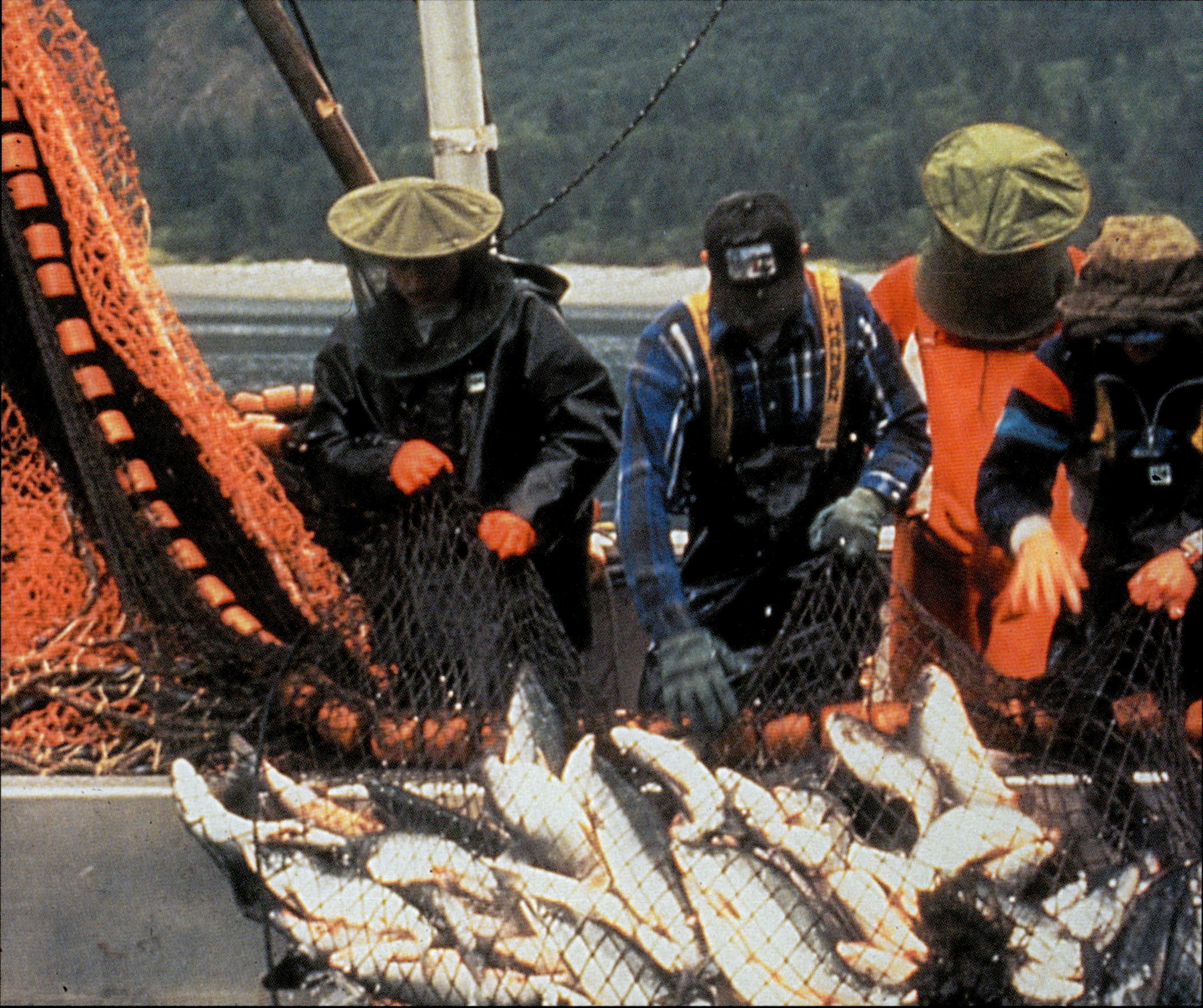
Photo by NOAA/Department of Commerce

© Ecoscene

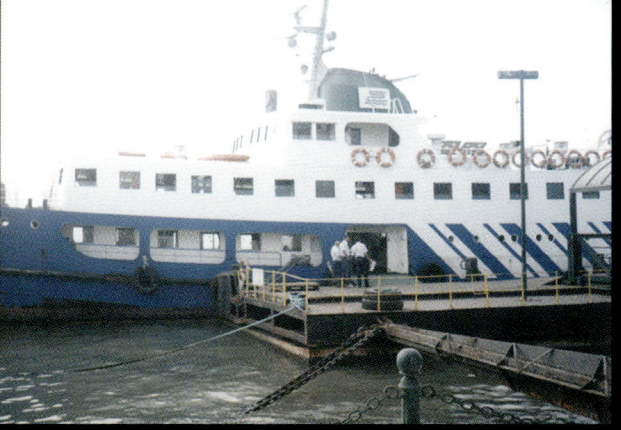

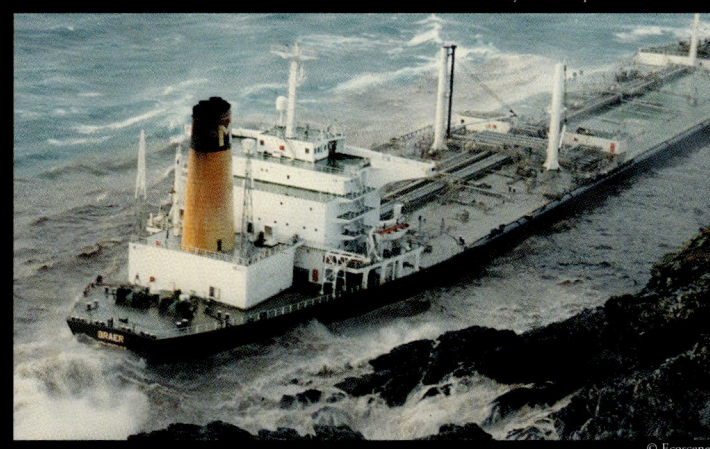

This book serves mainly as a text for the Project AWARE Specialty course, however it's also a valuable resource for anyone interested in understanding and preserving aquatic environments. In upcoming chapters you'll learn about:

- How the entire aquatic world functions as a single ecosystem (Chapter 2).
- The importance of and threats to both temperate and polar waters. (Chapter 3).
- Threats to one of the ocean's most spectacular environments — coral reefs (Chapter 4).
- The pertinent issues that place aquatic ecosystems in jeopardy, including fisheries concerns, coastal zone and wetlands degradation and pollution (Chapter 5).
- The world's most environmentally threatened aquatic regions (Chapter 6).
- Possible solutions to many aquatic environments' problems (Chapter 7).
- How you can help conserve worldwide aquatic ecosystems (Chapter 8).

HOW TO USE THIS BOOK

To get the most out of this book, first find a comfortable place that allows you to focus on what you're reading. Next, skim through the book, noting headings, photos, illustrations and captions. This gives you an overview of what you'll be learning. When you begin a chapter, review the Study Questions. Look for the answers to these questions as you read. Highlighting or underlining the answers in your book reinforces learning and helps you remember the information.

You'll find a short quiz at the end of each chapter that lets you assess your comprehension. If you miss any questions, review that part of the chapter until you understand the information. At the end of the book, you'll find a Knowledge Review that covers material from all chapters. Complete the Knowledge Review, rereading sections as necessary to find the answers. If you are enrolled in a Project AWARE Specialty course, your instructor will review the Knowledge Review with you and answer any additional questions you may have.

PADI – THE PROFESSIONAL ASSOCIATION OF DIVING INSTRUCTORS
"THE WAY THE WORLD LEARNS TO DIVE"

PADI (Professional Association of Diving Instructors) is the world's largest recreational diver training organization. The PADI membership includes dive businesses, resort facilities, academic institutions, instructor trainers, dive educators, divers, snorkelers and other watersports enthusiasts. Professional PADI Members (dive centers, resorts, educational facilities, instructors, assistant instructors and divemasters) teach the vast majority of the world's recreational divers, issuing nearly 1,000,000 certifications each year. PADI Professionals make underwater exploration and adventure accessible to the public while maintaining the highest industry standards for dive training, safety and customer service. PADI was the first training organization to establish a nonprofit organization dedicated to preserving the aquatic environment, the Project AWARE Foundation

PROJECT AWARE

When it comes to the health of our aquatic environment, no community has such a personal view or cares more passionately than divers. Responding to the growing awareness of the problems facing both ocean and freshwater ecosystems, PADI founded Project AWARE (Aquatic World Awareness, Responsibility and Education) in 1989. Project AWARE seeks to increase, through education, the recreational dive community's environ-mental awareness, and to encourage responsible interaction between humans and the aquatic environment.

Each year, Project AWARE exposes nearly one million people to aquatic education programs, responsible dive practices and conservation efforts through its worldwide network of more than 100,000 PADI Professionals.

Project AWARE's Purpose and Mission

Project AWARE's mission, as indicated by its name, is based on three goals: awareness, responsibility and education. Project AWARE exists to:

- Cultivate interest in and support for programs and initiatives within the environmental and dive community that preserve the aquatic environment and its resources.
- Teach the world about the importance of and our responsibility for preserving the aquatic environment.
- Develop and disseminate educational materials to create public awareness.

Since its inception, with support from PADI Offices, professionals and divers worldwide, Project AWARE has worked to promote and organize environmental efforts, as well as provide financial support to worthwhile aquatic conservation and preservation endeavors. To strengthen our common goals and reinforce a widespread commitment to the aquatic environment, Project AWARE has joined forces, built alliances and formed partnerships with like-minded civic and governmental organizations.

Project AWARE Specialty Course

In 1998, Project AWARE expanded its educational mission by introducing the Project AWARE Specialty course. This course is a formal, but fun, introduction for divers and nondivers alike to the plight of the world's aquatic ecosystems. Committed PADI Professionals offer this program to *anyone* who wants to find out more about, and take responsibility for, marine and freshwater environments. Although diving and snorkeling offer the best avenues to appreciate the aquatic world, you do not have

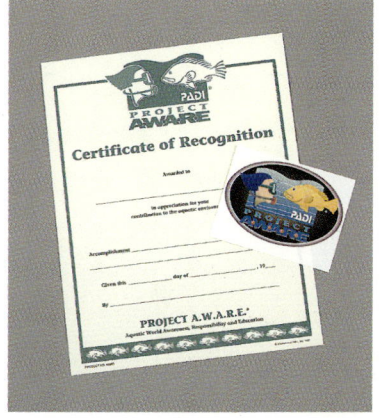

to dive to participate in the Project AWARE Specialty course – it's open to everyone. The only requirement is an interest in learning more about the 70 percent of the earth covered with water.

Project AWARE Foundation

Much of Project AWARE's mission is carried out through the Project AWARE Foundation, the dive industry's leading nonprofit environmental organization. The Foundation funds and assists projects that enrich humanity's awareness and understanding of the aquatic world. It also supports environmental research, educational efforts, and legislative initiatives aimed at managing and conserving aquatic resources.

Through its micro and macro grant programs, Project AWARE Foundation, along with affiliated international Project AWARE Charities, distributes more than $300,000 US annually. This number

International Cleanup Day Participants Tabulating Trash

Diver Participating In an Underwater Monitoring Project

A Diver Installing a Mooring Buoy to Protect a Reef From Anchor Damage

continues to grow steadily each year. Individuals and groups apply for grants to fund efforts ranging from local dive site cleanups to long-term research projects.

Over the last decade, Project AWARE Foundation has contributed to the success of numerous environmental efforts. A few noteworthy contributions include:

- International Cleanup Day. Each September tens of thousands of divers and nondivers clean above and below the water at local shorelines as part of a global effort. Working with the Center for Marine Conservation (CMC), cleanup organizers record the amount and types of trash they recover. This data is compiled by CMC and used to monitor improvements in certain areas or decline in others.

- Dive Into Earth Day. On Earth Day, 22 April, Project AWARE supporters around the world organize and conduct special environmental projects and events. These efforts include underwater cleanups, mooring buoy installations, reef survey projects, fish counts or other ecological programs that educate divers and encourage positive interaction with the aquatic environment.

- Artificial Reefs and Wrecks. Since the early 1990s, the Foundation has helped turn several ships into artificial reefs off the Canadian, Mexican and US coasts, and in the North American Great Lakes. Organizers thoroughly clean the ships and open many passageways to make them appealing to marine life as habitat and safer for visiting divers before they go down. These artificial reefs help take pressure off of natural reefs that are in decline.

- Mooring Buoy Program. With the Foundation's help, hundreds of mooring buoys now float over many of the world's most popular dive sites,

© Michel Verdure

eliminating or reducing the need for dive boats to anchor. Anchor damage has stopped in some areas and is greatly minimized in others. Interested dive operators may receive complete instructions, consultation and financial support for installing buoys at local dive sites through the Foundation's program.

- Public Awareness Campaigns. Every year, the Project AWARE Foundation develops a public awareness campaign focusing on a specific aquatic creature, area or problem. Campaign elements include creation of brochures, posters, stickers, lapel pins, articles for publication and public service announcements for distribution to dive centers, aquariums, schools and television stations. Through promotion of a unified message, these campaigns increase worldwide interest in aquatic conservation efforts and attract many people to diving.

Environmental Efforts

Millions of certified divers and more than 100,000 PADI Professionals worldwide support and enhance Project AWARE initiatives. As the world's largest diver training organization, PADI encourages all student divers to protect the areas where they dive and to dive responsibly. PADI courses and programs promote environmentally sound dive practices, especially buoyancy control, and emphasize aquatic-life awareness and conservation. In addition PADI produced the *Ten Ways a Diver Can Protect the Underwater Environment* brochure which highlights simple efforts divers can make in their everyday

Photo by Claire Ellis

dive practices.

Prior to Project AWARE, divers were not always as cautious or conscious about their interactions with the environment. Gauge hoses dragged and bumped into delicate creatures. Careless fins and hands kicked, grabbed and broke fragile corals. Today, through the influence of environmental education, most divers take great care to streamline their equipment and monitor their movements to avoid contact with sensitive aquatic life.

As a business entity, PADI's corporate offices ensure that business operations and production practices are environmentally friendly. This includes reducing the use of styrofoam and other plastics, and recycling as much paper, aluminum and plastic as possible. PADI Offices make it a point to purchase recycled materials and products when practical.

PADI Dive Centers and Resorts are also encouraged to operate in an environmentally conscious manner and to promote environmental conservation whenever possible. Many dive operations ask customers to pick up trash as a regular activity during all dives.

Jointly, Project AWARE and PADI support specific ongoing lobbying efforts and legislative actions to help manage sustainable fisheries, protect endangered habitats and species and establish marine parks and other protected areas. For example, in 1999, Project AWARE Foundation provided official comment to the US Congress on a resolution (H. Con. Res. 189), which was eventually passed, banning shark finning in US waters. The Foundation, with strong support from PADI Professionals and divers, continues to help establish management plans for many marine sanctuaries and protected areas worldwide.

CHAPTER TWO
THE AQUATIC WORLD—ONE BIG ECOSYSTEM

EARTH'S AQUATIC ENVIRONMENT

THE AQUATIC WORLD — ONE BIG ECOSYSTEM

- **EARTH'S AQUATIC ENVIRONMENT**
- **FRESHWATER ECOSYSTEMS**
- **THE OCEAN AND SEAS**
- **MARINE PRODUCTIVITY**
- **THE COASTAL ZONE**

STUDY QUESTIONS
Underline/highlight the answers to these questions as you read:
1. How is all water on earth ultimately connected?
2. How do aquatic regions compare to land regions in terms of size, area, living space and temperature?
3. What are the two primary freshwater ecosystems and what distinguishes them?
4. What are the two primary ocean zones and what are their distinguishing features?
5. What is the average mineral (salt) composition of the ocean and where does it come from?
6. What is the base of the marine food chain, and why are some areas much more productive than others?
7. How does the productivity of coastal and open ocean environments differ?
8. What makes the coastal zone and wetlands so important?

Although we talk about the world's "oceans" in the plural, there is really only one ocean. In fact, all water on earth is ultimately connected. Despite separation and confinement by land, all aquatic systems — fresh and saltwater – are linked.

The ocean's five different names (Pacific, Atlantic, Antarctic, Arctic and Indian) came about at a time when humans knew little of earth's geography. Today, these names serve as a convenient way to identify different areas of one ocean.

It may appear that freshwater accounts for a sizable portion of the earth's *hydrosphere* (or aqueous envelope around the earth, including bodies of water) – but it doesn't. All the water contained in North America's Great Lakes, Russia's Lake Baikal, South America's Amazon River, Africa's Nile River, China's Yellow River and the United States' Mississippi River combined do not come close to the amount of water in the Indian Ocean basin. Only about three percent of all water on earth is fresh and three-quarters of that is frozen in the polar ice caps. Another 20 percent is ground water. That leaves very little water to account for the numerous rivers, streams and lakes of the world. Yet, this relatively small amount is incredibly important to life on earth.

No matter where it is — and whether it's fresh or salt — water is water. It is two atoms of hydrogen joined with one atom of oxygen. Through the hydrologic cycle of continual evaporation, condensation and precipitation, every drop eventually circulates through every ocean, sea, bay, river, lake or stream. The water in the ocean today may have been in a river yesterday. It could also have been part of an ice cube in someone's freezer or pumped up from a deep well and deposited on someone's lawn.

As water carries pollutants with it as it cycles around, the potential for damage spreads. This is why water quality issues are a global, rather than regional concern.

Size, Area and Living Space

Water covers more than 70 percent, or 365,656,200 square kilometres/141,180,000 square miles of the globe. The Pacific Ocean alone is 25 percent larger than all land areas com-bined. By volume, the ocean contains 1350 million cubic kilometres/324 million cubic miles of water, accounting for more than 99 percent of all living space on earth.

Besides dominating the earth's surface, the ocean hides another surprise — its incredible depth. While the average land elevation is 840 metres/2755 feet, the average ocean depth is about 3729 metres/12,238 feet. The deepest depth is found in an area known as Challenger Deep in the Pacific

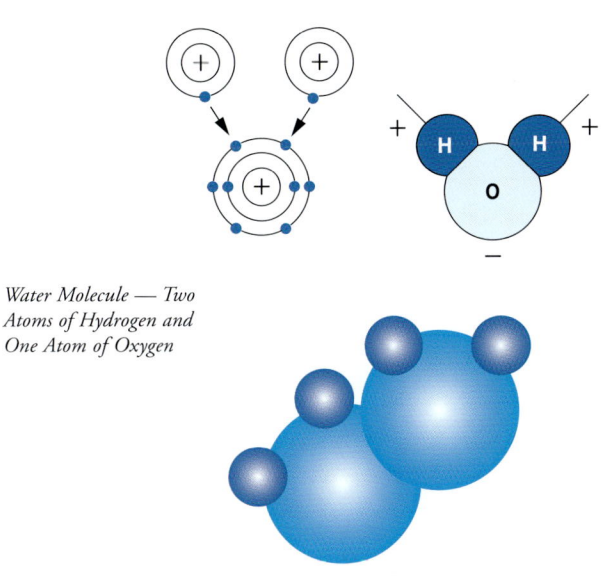

Water Molecule — Two Atoms of Hydrogen and One Atom of Oxygen

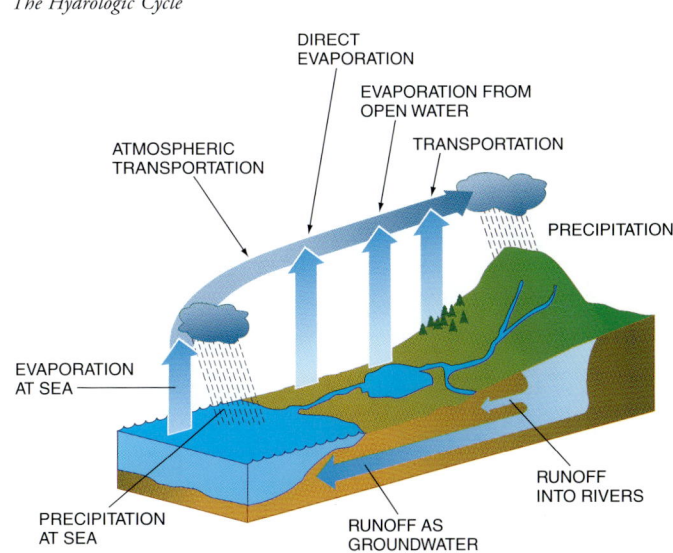

The Hydrologic Cycle

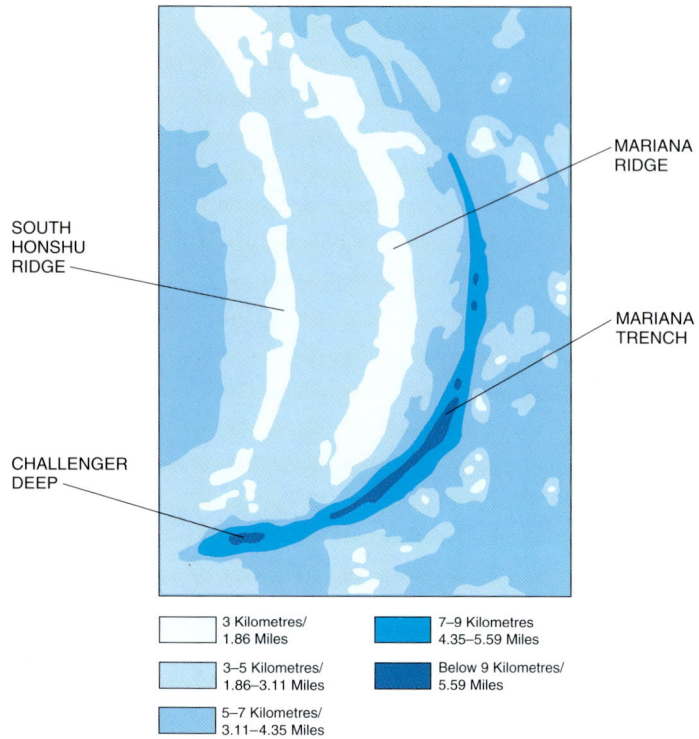

Relief Map Showing the Relative Depths of the Mariana Trench and its Surroundings

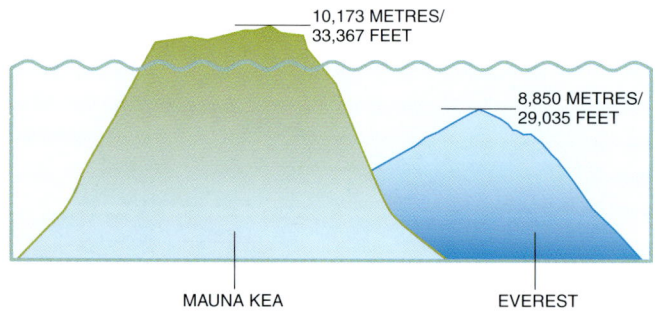

The Earth's Highest Mountain, Mauna Kea, as Compared to Mount Everest

Ocean's Marianas Trench. This area was named after the British ship *Challenger* that first pinpointed the trench's location in 1951. Here, the bottom lies at 11,022 metres/36,150 feet — that's 11.02 kilometres/6.85 miles. At this depth you could completely submerge Mount Everest, the highest point on earth, and still have more than 2400 metres/8000 feet of water above it. The pressure at the bottom of the Marianas Trench is an astounding 1200 kilograms per square cent-imetre/16,000 pounds per square inch.

Even earth's highest mountain ranges pale in comparison to those that rest on the sea floor. For example, Mount Everest rises 8850 metres/29,028 feet above sea level, yet it's relatively small compared to Hawaii, USA's Mauna Kea. When measured from the sea floor, Mauna Kea stands 10,173 metres/33,367 feet, though only 4193 metres/13,753 feet stands above sea level.

The earth's longest mountain range is also underwater. The Mid-Ocean Ridge winds its way from the Arctic Ocean through the Atlantic, skirts the African, Asian and Australian continents and crosses the Pacific Ocean to the west coast of North America. That's four times longer than South America's Andes, North America's Rockies and Asia's Himalayan mountain ranges combined.

Temperature

Another vital distinction between water and land is temperature range. Terrestrial environments show incredible fluctuations, from nearly minus 37° C/100° F in Antarctica to well over 37° C/100° F in many parts of the world.

Aquatic temperatures are much more constant

photo by Jack Archibald

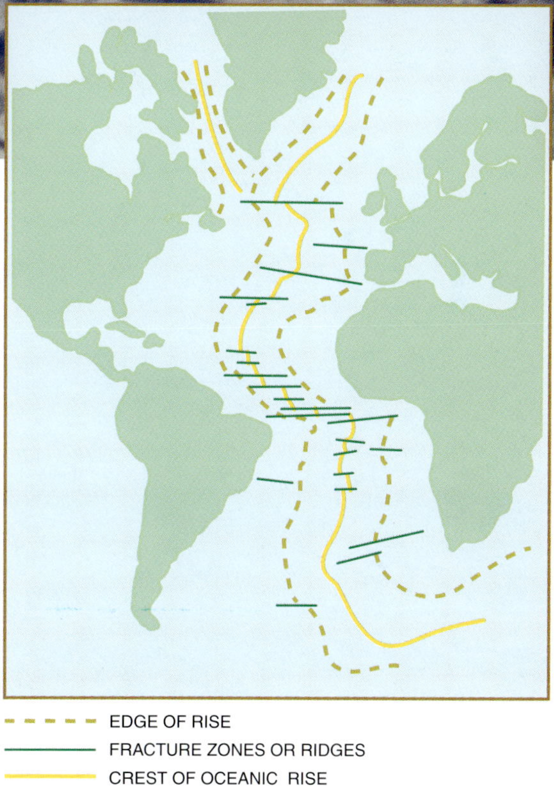

because water remains liquid only within a relatively narrow range, and can absorb more heat than any other naturally occurring substances. These factors make aquatic environments far more temperature stable than the terrestrial environment. As a result, aquatic ecosystems lack sharp daily fluctuations in temperature, causing gradual seasonal changes. This is especially true in the deep ocean.

Although the variation is far less than that on land, water surface temperatures can differ widely — from below freezing in polar regions (salt content prevents freezing) to 37° C/100° F in the Persian Gulf. However, the average water temperature in the deep ocean (comprising 99 percent of seawater) is a constant, bone-chilling 3.5° C/37° F.

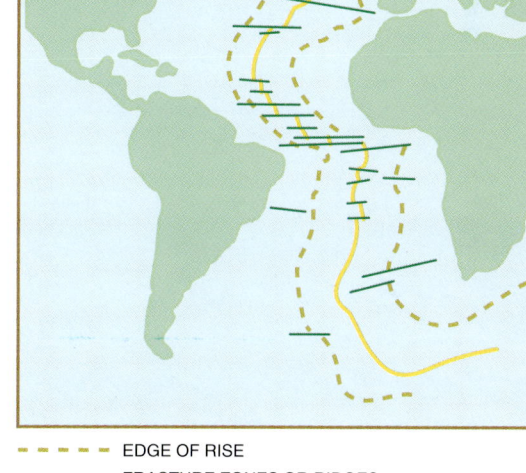

- - - EDGE OF RISE
— FRACTURE ZONES OR RIDGES
— CREST OF OCEANIC RISE

The Mid-Ocean Ridge in the Atlantic Ocean

19

Photo by NOAA/Department of Commer

FRESHWATER ECOSYSTEMS

While they account for only a tiny portion of earth's aquatic environments, freshwater ecosystems are varied and vitally important regions. There is no better example of freshwater ecosystem diversity than the Amazon River. Many scientists believe the Amazon to be the most diverse region, containing almost as many fish species as found on all coral reefs worldwide and five times more species than found on Caribbean reefs.

The movement of fresh water also provides an important function. It shapes landmasses by continual erosion and deposition. The sediment it carries nourishes plants and animals. The transportation it provides has helped shape human history.

Limnology, the study of freshwater ecosystems, is broadly divided into two groups:
Lentic – standing water habitats such as lakes and ponds,
Lotic – running water habitats such as rivers and streams.
Some wetlands, tidal flats or estuaries that contain much soil moisture, are also freshwater ecosystems.

Lentic Ecosystems

Lakes and ponds are essentially nothing more than inland depressions containing standing water. They vary from small ponds of less than one hectare/2.4 acres to large inland seas covering thousands of square kilometres/miles. They may be as shallow as one metre/three feet to more than 2000 metres/6000 feet.

Lakes and ponds form through glacial erosion and deposition, rock and debris accumulation blocking streams, or by earth movement that causes land to sink and flood. Some freshwater bodies form through nongeologic activity.

© Carol Haney

Humans intentionally dam rivers and streams for water storage, power and irrigation. Quarries and strip mines fill with water and even beavers dam up streams to make shallow but often extensive ponds.

Temperature gradients in lakes and ponds influence biological stratification. The *littoral zone* is the area near the lake margin where light penetrates to the bottom and rooted plants grow. Beyond this is the open water or *limnetic zone*, which is inhabited by plankton and fish. Below the depth of effective light penetration is the region termed the *profundal zone*. Here the diversity of life varies with temperature and oxygen supply.

The bottom is termed the *benthic zone*. Although it may not be apparent to the untrained eye, the bottom harbors intense biological activity created by the decomposition of organic matter. *Anaerobic* (no oxygen) bacteria dominate the bottom beneath the profundal water, whereas the littoral zone's bottom is rich in *aerobic* decomposing organisms.

The food chain of many lake ecosystems depends on *phytoplankton* (tiny, single-celled photosynthetic organisms), although some lakes also strongly depend on *detritus* (fine remains of plant or animal tissue). Most lakes are subject to

© Carol Haney

cultural eutrophication – the rapid addition of nutrients from sewage and industrial wastes. Cultural eutrophication has produced significant detrimental biological changes in many freshwater ecosystems.

While less diverse than marine ecosystems, many freshwater ecosystems are biologically rich. The earth's oldest and deepest lake is a good example. Lake Baikal in Siberia is 25 million years old and 1620 metres/ 5315 feet deep. It contains more than 20 percent of the world's unfrozen fresh water. More than 1500 species live in Lake Baikal or the nearby area. Perhaps the most surprising resident of the lake is the Baikal seal, one of the few species of seals living in fresh water.

Lotic Ecosystems

Rivers and streams – lotic ecosystems – exhibit a wide variety of physical and ecological characteristics. Naturally, the conditions near the source of a river differ from its mouth. There is also a gradient across a river due to temperature and depth changes, channel width, current velocity and bottom topography.

Changes in these physical conditions are reflected in the living organisms that inhabit the ecosystem. Because lotic ecosystems are subject to constant movement, they require a constant supply of nutrients from land-based sources to thrive.

Many rivers begin as small streams in shady forested regions. These streams strongly depend on detritus that is processed by a number of invertebrates – shredders, collectors or grazers.

TEMPERATURE STRATIFICATION IN FRESH WATER

Many lakes and ponds cycle through seasonal temperature stratification. The process begins in summer with the sun warming the water's surface. As the water warms, it becomes less dense and, therefore, lighter. This enables it to float on the colder, denser water beneath. Because of density differences, the water layers don't mix easily. The barrier between the layers is characterized by a steep and rapid decline in temperature known as the *thermocline*.

As air temperature falls in autumn, the surface water loses heat to the atmosphere through convection, conduction and evaporation. This causes the temperature of the surface water to drop and sink. Over time, the temperature becomes uniform from the top to the bottom of the lake. The water can now easily circulate, carrying oxygen and nutrients throughout the lake. This seasonal mixing is called *overturn*.

Due to water's unique physical properties, ice formation has some significant and unexpected effects on thermal stratification. As water cools it becomes more dense, but as the temperature reaches 4° C/39° F the density begins to *decrease*, making colder water lighter. This near-freezing, lighter water remains on the surface and as the temperature continues to drop, it freezes. (If this didn't happen, ice couldn't float.)

Interestingly, the water immediately beneath the ice may be warmed by solar radiation. Because the water is below 4° C/39° F, warming actually *increases* its density. This heavier water now drops to the bottom where it mixes with water warmed by heat conducted from bottom mud. As a result, a slight inverse stratification may develop, in which the water becomes warmer with depth.

As ice melts in spring, the surface water again reaches 4° C/39° F and begins to sink. This mixing, aided by the wind circulating water, is an important process because it frees bottom nutrients and mixes them with the oxygen-rich surface waters. This creates an ideal growing condition for plankton. As the season progresses, the summer stratification develops again.

These organisms, along with algae, slow the downstream movement of nutrients. As these streams grow and are exposed to sunlight, their dependence shifts from detritus to producing their own food from algae and rooted aquatic plants. As the river grows larger still, it shifts back to a dependence on detritus and dissolved organic matter.

Generally, downstream systems depend on the inefficiencies of nutrient processing upstream. What lives downstream survives on what's left over from upstream. However, this also means that pollutants that enter the system upstream may accumulate in downstream inhabitants.

THE OCEANS & SEAS

The ocean floor consists of the deep seabed and the continental margin. The continental margin includes the coastal region (beaches, marshes, estuaries and lagoons), the *continental shelf* and the *continental slope*. The *continental shelf*, as the name implies, is that portion of the sea floor adjacent to and surrounding land masses. This region accounts for 5.4 percent of the earth's total area. Shelf depths range from 20-500 metres/60-1650 feet, but the average is about 130 metres/426 feet. The continental shelf, termed the *neritic zone*, is very important in terms of biological productivity.

The shelf's gentle, smooth platform ends in an abrupt slope called the *shelf break*. Here it becomes the *continental slope*, which accounts for another 10.8 percent of the earth's surface area. The region beyond the continental slope is called the *deep ocean*, and this accounts for more than half — 54.6 percent – of the earth's surface area.

The ocean is made up of two zones: The *photic zone* (having to do with light), and the perpetual darkness or *aphotic zone*. The transition between these two zones is gradual, so the photic zone is defined as the depth to which one percent of surface light intensity is present. While the photic zone has enormous importance for life on earth, it represents a relatively small portion of the ocean. More than 90 percent of the deep ocean is well below the reach of light, within the aphotic zone — the area below 200 metres/640 feet.

Mineral Composition

Given some slight variation, seawater contains about 3.5 percent dissolved inorganic material (salts), made up of all the elements and compounds found in the earth's crust. In fact, if all the salt was extracted from the ocean and piled up on land, it might cover the continents to a depth of 1.5 metres/5 feet. If gold could be extracted, every person on the planet would have about four kilograms/nine pounds.

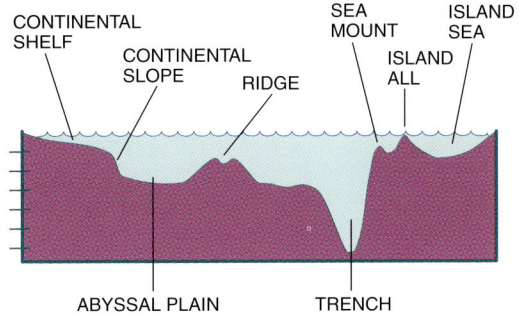

Cross Section of the Sea Floor Showing Major Topographical Features

Dissolved salts enter the ocean primarily from river outflow, although deep sea *hydrothermal vents* — cracks in the ocean floor that spew forth mineral rich, extremely hot fluids — also contribute to salinity. It's estimated that rivers carry up to 16 billion metric tons/18 billion tons of sediment into the sea each year, of which about 2.9 billion metric

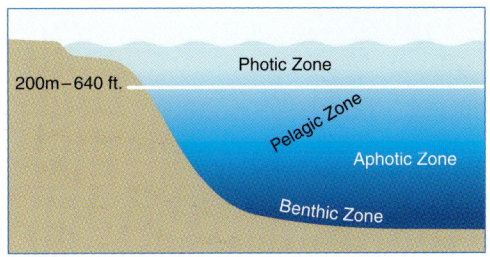

The Continental Shelf and Slope Showing the Ocean's Major Zones

tons/3.2 billion tons are dissolved salts. The river adding the greatest amount of sediment each year is China's Yellow River, which contributes 1.6 billion metric tons/1.8 billion tons annually, followed by India's Ganges River at 1.3 billion metric tons/1.4 billion tons.

MARINE PRODUCTIVITY

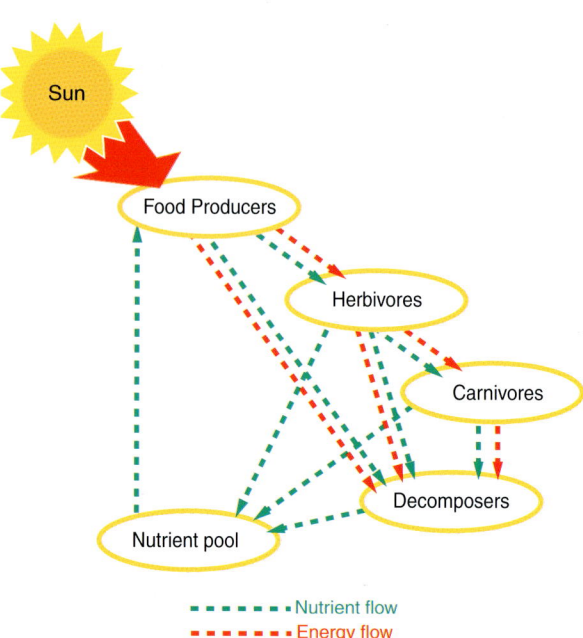

The Marine Food Chain

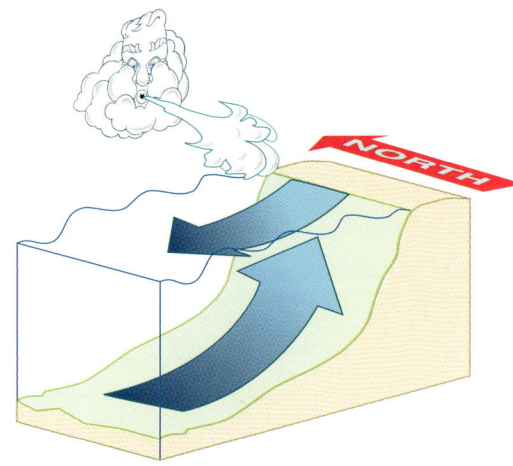

Upwelling Along a Shoreline in the Northern Hemisphere

Although it varies according to water clarity, in general, there is too little light below about 200 metres/650 feet to support photosynthesis. This barrier defines where *phytoplankton* flourish. Phytoplankton provide food for the next rung on the food chain, *zooplankton*. Zooplankton, animal plankton (in Biology, the prefix zoo- denotes something related to animals), feed larger creatures, like fish. Thus, the world's major fishing areas generally follow the pattern of phytoplankton production.

While light is essential for productivity, it's not all that's required - nutrients are also vital. However, because most nutrients lie on or near the sea bottom — often within the aphotic zone — there must be a way for them to reach the life-giving photic zone. Water circulation accomplishes this. Nutrients reach the surface in abundance in areas of coastal upwelling, where deeper, more nutrient-rich waters rise to take the place of warmer surface waters driven away by offshore winds or surface currents.

Upwelling is why areas off the coasts of Peru, California and West Africa are so productive, and have traditionally supported major fisheries. Likewise, the shallow waters of most continental shelves generally have high production because nutrients enter from land-based sources such as rivers and estuaries. Polar regions are moderately productive because currents and winds mix the water.

The coastal zone and areas of upwelling produce

CORIOLIS, UPWELLING AND EL NINO

How exactly does upwelling bring nutrient-rich bottom water to the surface? Upwelling is the primary mechanism and this is dependent upon the Coriolis effect. Simply stated, the Earth's rotation causes surface currents in the ocean to deflect to the right in the Northern Hemisphere and to the left in the Southern Hemisphere. The exact mechanism of the Coriolis effect is beyond the scope of this book, but it has a very important consequence near the continental shelves on the eastern sides of oceans. In the Northern Hemisphere winds blowing from the north deflect surface waters to the right, or toward the west. As water is moved offshore, it is replaced by water from underneath. This process is called upwelling. On occasion, in the southern Pacific, this trend is reversed and an El Nino occurs. In an El Nino pattern, surface water is pushed towards the coast rather than away from it. Because many productive fisheries are centered on these upwelling areas, an El Nino year can spell disaster for many fishermen in countries such as Peru.

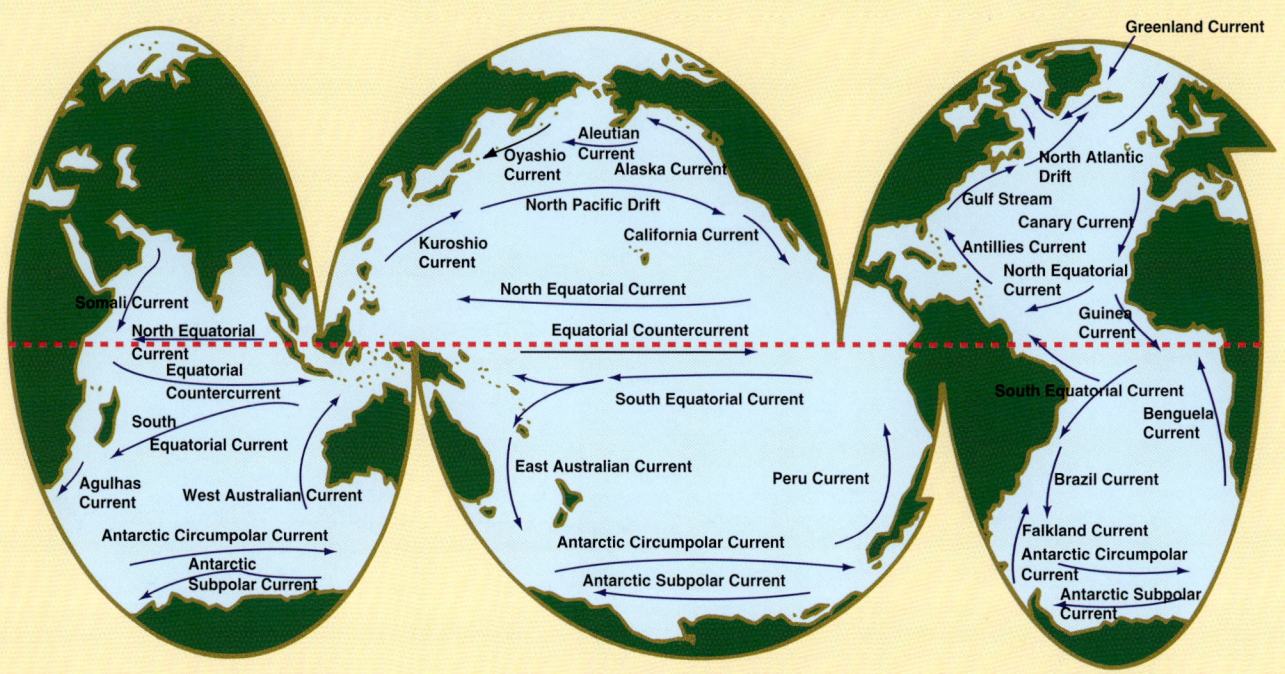

Currents – The Rivers in the Sea

The Ocean's water is constantly in motion, but there is a pattern and direction to this seeming chaos. Benjamin Franklin noticed this when he spoke of the Gulf Stream as a river in the sea. Currents can be global, such as the Antarctic Circumpolar Current, or localized, such as the Florida Current and occur in all ocean depths. Surface currents are currents present in the upper 10 percent of the water and derive mainly from wind patterns.

Wind is driven by differences in solar heating across the surface of the earth. This wind then has a direct effect on the direction of motion in the water. Combined with the Coriolis effect, large amounts of water are moved in circular patterns called gyres – to the right in the Northern Hemisphere and to the left in the Southern Hemisphere. There are six major gyres, the North Atlantic and the North Pacific in the Northern Hemisphere and the South Atlantic, the South Pacific, the Indian Ocean and the Antarctic Circumpolar Current in the Southern Hemisphere. Although less influential than wind, solar heating also effects currents. At the poles, water is cooled, becoming less salty and denser. This water then "flows" downward towards the equator.

Currents also persist below the upper layer of the ocean and are driven primarily by thermohaline circulation. This process is responsible for most vertical water movement and eventually circulates the entire ocean. This circulation starts because equatorial regions receive more heat than polar regions. Simplistically, water is cooled and made denser and less salty at the poles. This water then sinks and drifts towards the equator. As the water moves towards the equator, it is warmed and made less dense, therefore rising to the surface. Once on the surface it is pushed again towards the poles where it is cooled and the process begins anew.

The Sea's Wayward Wanderers — Plankton

The word plankton is taken from the Greek verb meaning "to wander". These wandering organisms are pelagic (living above the bottom) life forms carried around by water movement rather than their own ability to swim. Although some species are weak swimmers, the vast majority cannot swim actively against even the weakest current.

Plankton are divided into two basic groups - phytoplankton, or plant plankton and zooplankton, or animal plankton. Perhaps you've never actually seen plankton, but if you've ever gone scuba diving or swimming at night, you've probably seen the tiny sparks or light, or bioluminescence, many planktonic species give off when disturbed.

Most planktonic organisms are very small or microscopic. But there are exceptions. Although most people think of the blue whale as the longest aquatic organism, this title actually goes to a planktonic organism called a siphonophore. Siphonophores are colonies of small, very delicate organisms similar to jellyfish. Individual siphonophore colonies have been measured longer than 30 metres/100 feet. Other large planktonic organisms include the floating Man-o-War jellyfish that can have tentacles as long as 15 metres/50 feet.

Plankton comprise the largest group of organisms in the ocean. Jellyfish, small shrimp and crab-like animals, tiny worms, microscopic plants and floating seaweed all belong to this group. Some species remain planktonic their entire lives, while others begin life as planktonic larval forms that later mature into larger organisms. Lobsters, crabs and some fish are all examples of organisms with planktonic juvenile stages during their life cycle.

Although they are often looked over, plankton might just be the most important life form on Earth. Through photosynthesis, phytoplankton convert water and carbon dioxide into organic material — food. They are at the base of the oceanic food chain and without them few other life forms in the ocean could exist. Besides being a food source, phytoplankton also manufacture a large portion of the Earth's oxygen.

Clouds of phytoplankton can even be seen from the air. A sudden growth, or bloom, of distinct types of phytoplankton will discolor the water. Plankton blooms with a rust tint are called red tides. These red tides typically occur during periods of high sunlight and when concentration of nutrients such as phosphorus or nitrate are high, often from runoff. Red tides are made up primarily of dinoflagellates (a single-celled algae). These dinoflagellates produce neurotoxin that can be detrimental to other organisms in the area. Red tides also cut down on visibility underwater and have been known to cause other aquatic disturbances.

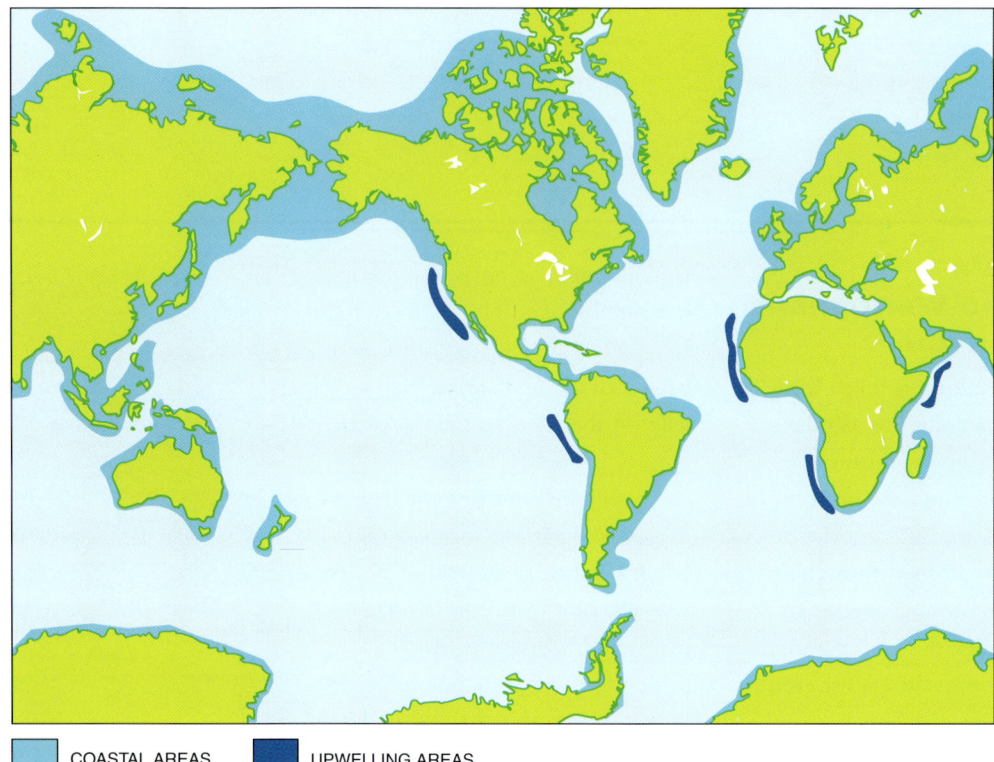

The World's Most Productive Fishing Areas

COASTAL AREAS   UPWELLING AREAS

slightly less than 50 percent of the world's fish catch. About 98 percent of the global fish catch is taken within 300 kilometres/984 miles of shore, which explains why many countries protect their 320 kilometre/200 mile limit (economic zone). This allows them to control fishing in these areas. In addition, about 90 percent of all marine life is concentrated along the coastal margins.

While the open ocean makes up about 90 percent of the total ocean, less than one percent of fish are caught there. Compared to shallow coastal waters, the deep ocean is a biological desert, except in certain areas near hydrothermal vents. Likewise, tropical waters are also very low in nutrients and plankton, explaining why these waters are so clear.

The sea yields more than just marine life. The oceans are also rich in minerals. Saltwater is a source of boron, bromine, calcium, magnesium, potassium, sodium, sulfur and uranium. Sediments on the continental shelf and slope yield sand, gravel, phosphorite, lime and silica. In addition, these sediments contain heavy minerals like magnetite, rutile, zircon, cassiterite, chromate, monazite and gold. The mud of the continental shelf and slope are rich in copper, lead, silver, zinc, oil, gas and sulfur.

Even the deep ocean is a potential source of raw material. Various chemical processes cause the formation of manganese nodules on the deep ocean floor. But these nodules contain more than just manganese – they also yield copper, nickel and cobalt. At the present, though, there are tremendous practical and legal problems that must be solved before these deep-water mineral reserves can be used to their full potential.

THE COASTAL ZONE

The coastal zone is defined as "the land-sea-air interface" around continents and islands extending from the inland limit of tidal influence to the outer extent of the continental shelf. It's important to note that much of what influences the coastal zone is the watershed draining into coastal areas, which can extend hundreds or even thousands of kilometres/miles inland. These regions are interrelated, interdependent and encompass multiple ecosystems as well as legal jurisdictions. This helps explain why coastal zone management is a complex and difficult process. However, the idea of integrated coastal zone management has come about to combat some of these complexities. One good example of integrated coastal zone management in action is the Partnerships in Environmental Management for the Seas of East Asia Project, or PEMSEA. A cooperative effort, PEMSEA supports the efforts of 11 participating governments in the East Asia region to prevent and manage marine pollution at the national and regional levels on a long-term basis. This program involves all stakeholders to eliminate marine debris from both land- and ocean-based sources. The group makes use of numerous integrated coastal management approaches and has so far implemented such programs in China and the Philippines. The success of the PEMSEA organization and the programs it fosters is evidence that integrated coastal zone management is an effective way to manage coastal and marine resources. The program's next phase will extend initiatives throughout East Asia.

The interface between land and sea is a tremendous place. Not only is it one of the most beautiful and dramatic areas, it is also one of the most complex. Because of the

numerous factors which act on this region and its intrinsic characteristics and importance, coastal zone management is now a common occurrence around the world.

The coastal zone is important to people because it is one of the most productive areas and gives rise to numerous plant and animal species, some of which form a large proportion of the human diet. In addition, the fishing and other resource collection industries also provide economic benefits. For those living at the coast, the coastal zone provides a buffer to the storms, surf and other climate changes that threatened livelihood and well-being. For those so inclined, the coastal zone is also a large playground for activities centered on, in and around the water.

However, the coastal zone in all of its beauty and importance faces ominous pressure in the form of both human-induced activity and natural processes. These natural processes are simply the way of the coast and include wind, waves, storms and surge among others. These natural processes reshape the coastal zone continuously. However, it is the human-induced activities that give rise to the need for coastal zone management. The intrinsic beauty of the coastal zone also causes some problems. In the United States alone, the coastal zone encompasses only 10 percent of the land mass, but houses nearly one-half of the nation's residents. The infrastructure necessary to support such a population places tremendous pressure on the natural environment. Runoff from urban areas is one of the greater problems for coastal zone managers and large populations only exacerbate these effects. In addition, humans often alter the natural topography to suit their development needs, building seawalls, jetties and groins.

The need for management of the coastal zone occurs when these natural processes come into conflict with these human, or social, processes. While the popularity of the coastal zone has increased, the available resource base and natural processes have remained the same. However, the nature of this zone renders management through governments difficult. Often, jurisdictions overlap and conflict. In addition, the coastal zone is often affected by processes occurring well inland, up in the watershed. The large areas affected, the overlapping jurisdiction and the strong interest of other stakeholder groups such as fishermen, business and real-estate developers and residents present a troubling management picture for the future. However, collaboration of management and stakeholders with the goal of sustainable coastal zone management promises hope for the continued enjoyment of this vital land-sea interface.

Coastal Wetlands

Because of their importance as habitats and food sources, some coastal ecosystems, such as mangrove forests, salt marshes and estuaries, are especially crucial for food production. In fact, two-thirds of the world's fisheries directly depend on the fertility of these regions because it is here that fish lay their eggs and juvenile fish develop.

Mangrove forests are the primary habitat fringing tropical and sub-tropical coastal regions. In temperate regions, salt

© Bret Forbes

© NOAA/Department of Commerce

marshes dominate this environment. Both mangroves and salt marshes require relatively wave-free conditions — often termed "low energy areas" — along tidal river banks, behind barrier beaches or at the shore end of wide lagoons.

Salt marsh and mangrove forest productivity is based on the microbial breakdown of plant matter by bacteria and fungi. This decaying organic matter — detritus — serves as the basis for an elaborate food chain. Mangroves' intricate root systems provide habitats for a host of invertebrates such as mussels, sponges, tunicates, hydroids and oysters, as well as the juvenile stages of many fish.

Wetlands are especially productive, often yielding as much as 3.6 metric tons/four tons per year of organic matter per hectare/acre. In comparison, a wheat field produces only about 0.36 metric tons/0.40 tons per year per hectare/acre, while the open ocean produces less than half of a wheat field's yield.

Another vital wetland function is the role of "waste treatment facility." Through microbial decay, wetlands remove many pollutants and process land-based nutrients that, especially in tropical regions, can adversely affect marine ecosystems.

Like wetlands, *estuaries* are generally nutrient-rich. An estuary is a partially enclosed body of water formed where

fresh water from a river or stream flows into the ocean and mixes with salt water. The nutrients flowing from an estuary support large populations of phytoplankton that, in turn, support more varied populations of marine life, such as fish and shellfish. As a result, more than 50 percent of commercially valuable fish spend part or all of their life cycle in estuaries. This makes these areas some of the most biologically productive marine regions on earth.

In addition, many other commercially important organisms such as oysters, clams and bay scallops spend their entire lives within estuaries. Estuaries are also a vital stop-over on the migration route of species like salmon and striped bass, and some eels. While some fish species breed in estuaries, others use it as a postnatal nursery area. For example, cod, herring and sole spawn in open ocean areas, but their young migrate to estuaries and return to the open ocean only when large enough to survive.

Freshwater Wetlands

Freshwater wetlands are closely associated with lakes and streams. The primary difference is that in wetlands, the water is at, near, or above ground level and occupied by water-loving vegetation. Wetlands dominated by grasses are *marshes*. Those dominated by woody vegetation are swamps.

Wetlands primarily consisting of accumulated peat (undecomposed or slightly decomposed material) are mires. Mires fed by water moving through the mineral soil and dominated by sedges are fens.

Wetlands dominated by sphagnum moss and dependent on precipitation for moisture and nutrients are bogs. Some

form of blocked drainage, an accumulation of peat and low productivity characterize bogs.

By contrast, marsh ecosystems don't operate like bogs at all. Instead of closing off the flow of nutrients, marsh vegetation acts as a nutrient "pump," drawing nutrients from the soil and making them readily available to the ecosystem.

Quiz

1. True or False. There are five geographically distinct oceans.
2. By area, more than _____ of the globe is covered by water and land accounts for _____ of the total available living space.
    a. 50 percent/one percent
    b. 70 percent/one percent
    c. 85 percent/50 percent
    d. 98 percent/50 percent
3. True or False. The average temperature of the deep ocean is 3.5° C/37° F.
4. Lakes and ponds are classified as _____ ecosystems and rivers and streams are called _____ ecosystems.
    a. photic / aphotic
    b. lentic / lotic
    c. aquatic / marine
5. The zone in the deep ocean that is well below the reach of light is called the:
    a. photic zone
    b. the continental shelf
    c. aphotic zone
    d. abyss
6. True or False. Seawater contains about 10 percent salt.
7. Tiny, single-celled photosynthetic organisms that form the base of the ocean's food chain are called:
    a. phytoplankton
    b. zooplankton
    c. fauna
    d. flora
8. True or False. Compared to productivity of shallow coastal waters, the deep ocean is a biological desert.
9. Coastal wetlands and estuaries are so important because: (choose all that apply)
    a. they supply nutrients that support large populations of phytoplankton.
    b. they host more than 50 percent of commercially valuable fish for part or all of their life cycle.
    c. many commercially important organisms such as oysters, clams and bay scallops spend their entire lives in estuaries.

How did you do? 1. False; 2. b; 3. True 4. b; 5. c; 6. False – it contains about 3.5 percent; 7. a; 8. True; 9. a, b and c.

CHAPTER THREE
TEMPERATE AND POLAR WATERS—
THE OCEAN'S FOUNDATION

TEMPERATE AND POLAR WATERS— THE OCEAN'S FOUNDATION

- **OCEAN PRODUCTIVITY**
- **LIFE BETWEEN THE TIDES**
- **KELP FORESTS**
- **POLAR REGIONS**

STUDY QUESTIONS
Underline/highlight the answers to these questions as you read:
1. What is primary productivity and what is the ocean's main source of productivity?
2. Why are there productivity peaks, or blooms, in the spring and fall in temperate waters?
3. What are the major hazards faced by intertidal organisms?
4. What is zonation in intertidal communities?
5. What three factors influence zonation in rocky intertidal habitat?
6. Why is kelp an important habitat?
7. What is a keystone species?
8. Why is productivity in the Southern Polar Ocean so great?
9. Why does the Arctic support more large animals than Antarctica?

Temperate water zones lie between 23-1/2 degrees and 66-1/2 degrees latitude while polar waters are those above 66-1/2 degrees latitude. But, the ocean doesn't have any physical boundaries and is in constant circulation, so temperate and polar zones are better defined through temperature.

Polar waters are rarely warmer than 10° C/50° F and can even be a bone-chilling -2° C/28° F at their coldest points. On the other hand, surface water in the temperate zones averages about 10° C/50° F; this region is particularly important to marine productivity because it forms the base of the food chain.

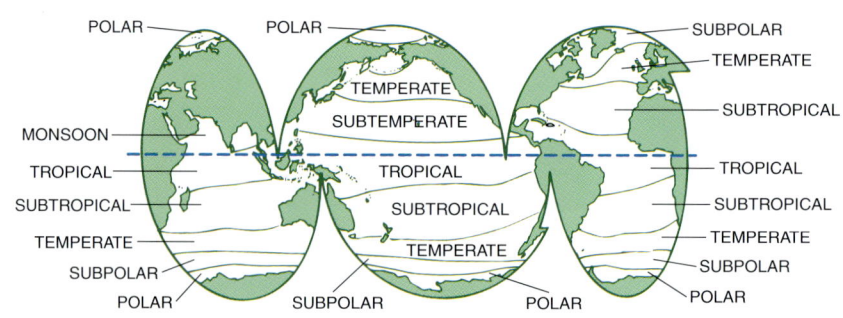

Global Marine Climatic Zones

OCEAN PRODUCTIVITY

*P*rimary productivity is the conversion of sunlight energy into chemical energy, or simply put, plant food. This process is called *photosynthesis*. Almost all major food webs are based on this primary productivity. The ocean's major source of productivity is *phytoplankton*. On land, productivity varies widely, but productivity in the ocean is much more even and consistent.

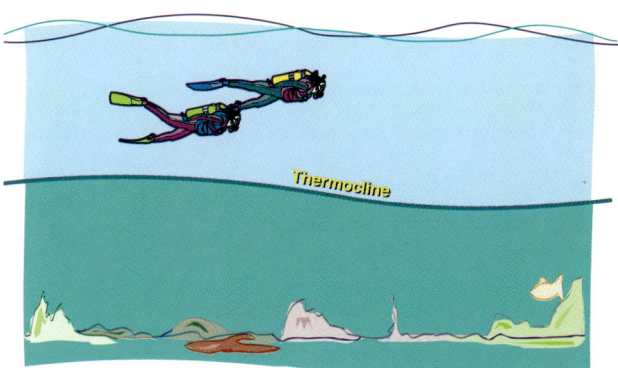

Thermal Stratification

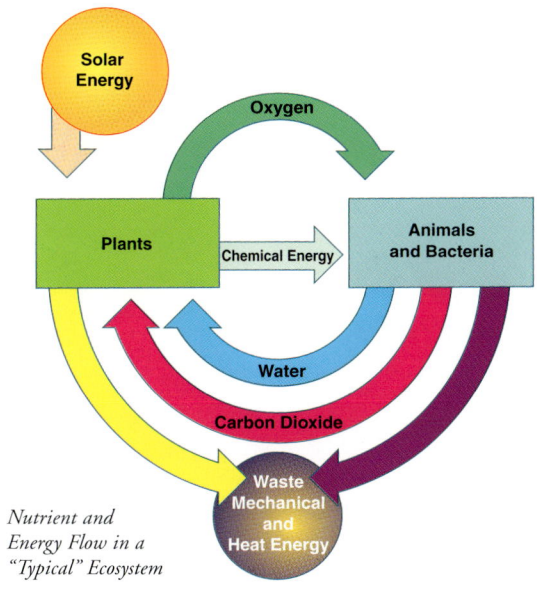

Nutrient and Energy Flow in a "Typical" Ecosystem

Temperate Seas

In temperate seas, the amount of sunlight entering the water varies seasonally, resulting in temperature fluctuations within the *photic zone*. Similar to freshwater ecosystems, these temperature changes alter the thermal structure (stratification) of the water column. During summer months, more sunlight hits the water and heats up the surface layer. This warm, less dense water covers a much colder and denser deep layer. The difference in density between the warmer and colder water results in a *thermal stratification*, such as the thermocline experienced by divers.

This stratification creates a barrier between the two layers and prevents any mixing. This prohibits the inorganic nutrients necessary for primary production from reaching the photic zone, rendering the overlying warm waters low in productivity.

However, the fall brings less solar energy and shorter days, which lessens the thermal stratification. Eventually, the temperature and density of the surface layer is little different from that of the underlying mass and mixing occurs whenever wind churns the waters. This lack of stratification also coincides with winter—the stormiest season—which further increases mixing. With the approach of spring and increasing solar energy, the surface temperatures again rise and a highly stratified water column is in place again by the summer.

In temperate seas, the productivity changes with the season. Typically, there is a major productivity peak in the spring (the "plankton bloom") and a lesser peak in the fall. Summer and winter both bring the lowest productivity, summer due to thermal stratification and winter due to a lack of sunlight. Therefore, the sea is most productive in the high latitudes, just equatorward of the Polar Regions.

Productivity in Coastal Waters

Productivity in coastal waters doesn't follow this simplified explanation precisely because localized factors have an important effect. Productivity is influenced by upwelling, which brings nutrient-rich waters to the surface and nutrient input from bays, rivers and streams. In addition, water covering the continental shelf (the *neritic zone*) is normally within the photic zone, which enables photosynthesis. Furthermore, shallow coastal regions don't usually show dramatic thermal stratification, so nutrients aren't usually locked up in bottom waters as they are elsewhere.

This means coastal productivity can remain high throughout the summer and is much greater than in oceanic regions. In addition, benthic plants and other nearshore ecosystems, such as seagrass beds, salt marshes and mangrove forests boost inshore primary productivity.

LIFE BETWEEEN THE TIDES

All coastal regions have an intertidal zone that depends on the tidal range. The tidal zone is one of Earth's harshest environments because organisms must be able to withstand both wet and dry conditions daily. In temperate zones, many coastlines have

significant tidal ranges (up to 12 metres/40 feet in Canada's Bay of Fundy), and intertidal communities are critical habitats.

Intertidal plants and animals have many adaptations allowing them to survive dry conditions at low tide. These include the ability to tightly clamp onto rocks, as with limpets; a shell closing its tight-fitting operculum, as seen in snails; or a retreat to tide pools, crevices or burrows to avoid heat and wind. When the tide returns, these organisms must be able to survive the transition to wet conditions and battering waves. To secure themselves, marine algae (seaweed) have tenacious structures called *holdfasts* attaching them to rocks. Some organisms, such as mussels, have specialized structures called *byssal threads* to secure themselves while oysters and barnacles cement themselves directly

How do tides occur?

Intertidal animals are capable of dealing with large fluctuations in their environment, but how exactly do these fluctuations arise? *Tides* are periodic short-term movements in the height of the ocean surface caused by a combination of the gravitational pull of the sun, the moon and the Earth's rotation. Since the moon is closer, its gravitational forces are the primary driving forces for tidal fluctuation. The moon literally pulls water towards it, creating a "bulge" facing the lunar surface. On the opposite side of the earth, another water "bulge" is created through lesser gravitational attraction. At right angles to the "bulges" are areas of less water. Since the water is pulled towards the moon, and opposite the moon, these depressions are created by a lack of water. As the earth rotates, a single point will move into a bulge of water, then into the corresponding depression. To an observer, the tide rises as the earth passes into a bulge, then recedes when the earth passes out of the bulge and into the depression.

The sun can also exert some effect on the strength of the tidal cycle. If the sun and moon are in line with the earth, the combined gravitational attraction is greater and results in a spring tide. However, if the moon and the sun are at right angles to each other, a neap tide occurs.

This explanation must also include some variation in tides due to land mass interference and basin shape. For these reasons, the Earth's actual tides are either semidiurnal (two high and two low tides of nearly equal intensity each day), diurnal (one high and one low tide each day) or mixed (successive high or low tides are of differing intensity).

to rocks with an adhesive they produce.

Intertidal zone residents also contend with predators, even at low tide. When exposed, intertidal zones are prime hunting grounds for seabirds and mammals.

In the intertidal zone, environmental conditions range from terrestrial, above the splash zone, to fully marine, below the lowest low tide. Most organisms occur within defined areas and this is called zonation. Zonation patterns are easily seen in the distribution of algae. Yellow, white, and gray lichens (a combination of fungi and bacteria) all live within the splash zone. Green seaweeds are common in the upper intertidal, while brown algae, including the ubiquitous *Fucus sp.*, are found closer to the water. Red seaweeds are easily found below the brown seaweed zone, and finally the large kelps are found in the subtidal zone.

Life Down Under

Although most people think of rocky shores as the intertidal, soft sediment communities are another prolific marine community. The minimal wave action along muddy shores allows rich organic matter to accumulate and this often supports dense gardens of marine plants. These plants can include both algae and true seagrasses. Unlike algae, seagrasses are flowering plants (*angiosperms*), whose ancestors once lived on land. One prominent and important temperate zone seagrass is eelgrass, which provides excellent habitat for grazing animals. These fast growing plants form the base of a rich and productive food web.

The soft-shore animal community is divided into two groups: the *epifauna*, or active surface-dwelling organisms, and *infauna* who spend their lives within the sediments.

Epifauna range from opportunistic feeders, such

as birds, to scavengers like crabs. In addition, these areas are sometimes called *marine nurseries* because the epifauna includes many juvenile organisms. In particular, many species of fish find estuarine habitat particularly protective during their juvenile years.

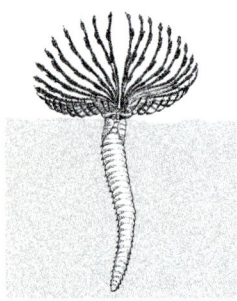

Benthic Infauna

The muddy shore's infauna must be resourceful to survive. Since the mud particles are so small and close together, these areas have little oxygen and animals have found different ways to obtain their oxygen. Burrowing animals like clams, extend snorkel-like siphons above the mud's surface while other residents create downwelling currents to circulate oxygen-rich water into the mud.

Life as a burrower requires both constructing a home in the mud and a way of collecting food. Some burrowers strain particles from the water using extended tentacles, while others plow through the sediments similar to an earthworm. Residents of the *interstitial* community are so small they actually live within the sediment, using the film of water surrounding individual sediment particles. These diverse and generally microscopic organisms feed on detritus and bacteria in the sediments.

Sandy shores are constantly moving high-energy zones and pose different problems for its inhabitants. Although seaweeds can't live in this area because there isn't any firm place for them to attach, interstitial animals can live between the sand particles. In addition, larger burrowing and filter feeding animals, such as clams, crabs, and some worms also thrive in the sandy shores.

Rocky Intertidal Shores

The extensive range and easy accessibility of the temperate ocean's rocky intertidal shores have permitted researchers to make many long-term direct observations and conduct experiments on community structure. As a result, we know more about the inhabitants and ecology of rocky shores than almost any other marine habitat.

The most noticeable characteristic of rocky shores is the grouping of plants and animals in distinctive patterns. This zonation is characteristic of all intertidal communities, but specific patterns and species vary depending upon location, tidal range and exposure to severe wave action. Of course, distinct zonation applies more to sessile (attached) species like algae, barnacles and mussels than mobile animals.

Encrusting black lichen, blue-green algae and a few primitive insects populate the rocky shore's splash or supralittoral zone. Just below this zone, periwinkles are unusually dense, with as many as 10,000 snails per square metre/8361 snails per square yard. Still lower in the intertidal are bands of barnacles with densities of thousands per square metre/square yard. Tightly congregated mussels often follow below the barnacles. This crowded existence creates intense competition among the animals for limited space.

But crowding does have its advantages. By forming tightly knit groups, these organisms establish microhabitats that can retain moisture during a low tide's dry spell. Also, since many sessile organisms, such as barnacles, need high population densities to mate, crowding also increases the likelihood of reproduction.

In addition to tidal levels, zonation in the rocky intertidal is influenced by various other factors. A

zone's upper range is often determined by physical factors. These include an organism's ability to withstand exposure to air, changing temperature and fluctuating salinity. A zone's upper limit can also be determined by biological factors such as the presence of suitable food or grazing pressure. The lower limit of a particular zone is normally limited by biological factors. Primary producers supporting rocky intertidal communities include benthic algae and phytoplankton, but this is a difficult environment for survival. Freezing temperatures and ice scouring limit algal production in the polar intertidal zones, but benthic algae reach their full potential in tem-perate climates.

Because these plants must compete for restricted space and sunlight, both physical and biological factors also determine benthic algae's zonation patterns. Upper limits are primarily determined by an algae's tolerance to exposure and drying, but grazing pressure is also important. And, humans can also affect the mix. For example, after the 1967 grounding of the *Torrey Canyon*, the dominant grazing mollusks in southwest England's intertidal zones were killed. Subse-quently, the upper zonation limits of several intertidal algae rose to occupy the now open space.

As the mollusk grazers recovered, they reduced the higher reaches of the algae and reestablished the original zonation pattern.

The intertidal's predator-prey relationships are complex. Limpets, chitons and sea urchins graze attached algae. Mussels, barnacles, clams, tunicates, sponges, and tubeworms filter water and depend upon plankton. Intertidal carnivores such as starfish eat limpets, snails, barnacles, mussels and oysters. Predatory snails consume a variety of prey, which can include clams, mussels and barnacles. Sea anemones prey on shrimp, small fish and worms while scavengers

abound. Shore birds are also significant predators when organisms are exposed during low tide.

Predation also controls the amount of primary production and type of benthic algae species in the rocky intertidal. Experiments have shown that removing grazing limpets or sea urchins both increased primary productivity and altered the species residing in the area.

Species composition and diversity of animals in the rocky intertidal are also determined through competition and predation. Mussels, barnacles and the carnivorous starfish, *Pisaster ochraceus*, dominate the rocky intertidal zone along North America's northwest pacific coast. This starfish feeds on a wide variety of mollusks and barnacles. When experimentally removed, the number of different species in the area was reduced from about 30 to one dominant mussel. *Pisaster* had been consuming the dominant mussel, thereby preventing its, or any other organism's, dominance in the community. *Pisaster* is called a *keystone species* because it has an effect on the number and type of species present in a community disproportionate to its numbers.

KELP FORESTS

In colder temperate regions, intertidal rocky shore communities give way to kelp forests in the subtidal zone. *Kelp* refers to a variety of large brown algae that grow where summertime water temp-eratures are about 20° C/68° F. They require a solid point of attachment, such as a rock, and form distinctive subtidal communities in areas exposed to fierce currents or heavy surf from depths of 20-40 metres/65-130 feet.

Kelp is widely distributed and is found off western coast of North and South America, Japan, northern China and Korea in the Pacific Ocean. In the Atlantic, there are large kelp beds off Canada's east coast, southern Greenland, Iceland and northern Europe. The southern ocean has kelp forests off the east coast of South America, the Falkland Islands, South Georgia Island and the South Sandwich Islands, as well as New Zealand, Southern Australia and South Africa.

Since kelp is an algae (not a flowering plant as found on land) they don't have roots, but attach to the bottom by holdfasts. Similarly, *stipe* and *blade* are used to describe the stalk and leaf, respectively. Some kelps also have *pneumatocysts*, or gas-filled floats, which keep

the blades near the surface of the water where they can photosynthesize. These kelp communities are highly productive because they have a large surface area for photosynthesis and there is a constant nutrient supply from the turbulent water.

Kelps are the largest of all algae and are among the fastest growing plants on earth. Most kelps grow from six to 25 centimetres/2.5 to 10 inches per day, but giant kelp (*Macrocystis pyrifera*) can grow as much as 50-60 centimetres/20-24 inches daily.

As with many other algae, kelps have a complex life cycle with two alternating generations. During the asexual phase, in which no male or female germ cell is produced, an adult *sporophyte* forms. Sporophyte offspring initiate the sexual reproductive phase by producing male and female *gametes* (equivalent to sperm and eggs). Asexual sporophytes quickly colonize a bare surface and develop into adults. During sexual reproduction, male and female gametes fuse to form a fertilized egg called a *zygote*. Sexual reproduction takes large amounts of energy, but the long-term evolutionary

Bull Kelp Life Cycle: A) Spores are Released from the Adult Plant, B) Spores Develop Into Sperm or Eggs, C) Fertilization is External and the Embryo Settles to the Bottom, D) The Embryo Grows into the Adult Sporophyte Stage

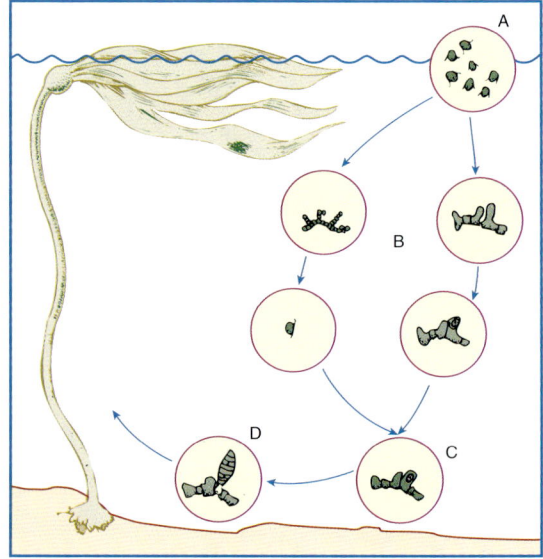

benefit is mixing of genes.

Kelp forests are extremely productive areas and the community in Alaska, USA's Aleutian Islands supported the Stellar sea cow (*Hydrodamalis gigas*). This gargantuan herbivore was the largest of all modern sirenia (the order that includes manatees and dugong), reaching eight metres/26 feet in length. But hunting by Russian fur traders resulted in its extinction a mere 27 years after its discovery in 1741. Kelp is also used extensively by humans who harvest more than 20,000 metric tons/-22,046 tons dry weight off the California coast each year. It is used for fertilizer, iodine salts and algin, a substance used as a thickener in products ranging from paint to whipped cream.

It is appropriate to call the kelp community a kelp forest. Like terrestrial forests, kelps are "rooted" to the bottom by their holdfast and spread up to reach sunlight. Also, the blades form a canopy that prevents light from reaching the bottom that provides habitat for shade-adapted algae.

Within this forest is also a diverse community of animals. Many species of algae have large blades that provide a platform for sessile communities such as smaller algae, diatoms, bryozoans and hydroids. Various worms, crustaceans and mollusks also wander over the blades while some sea slugs and other snails eat the kelp itself or feed on *epiphytic* algae growing on the surface of the larger kelp blades.

Kelp forests provide the food for herbivorous sea urchins, but the habitat also supports fish that feed on kelp forest residents or use it for shelter. Although kelp has been found in the stomach of some kelp forest fish species, researchers feel that this was accidental while the fish was hunting for prey on the algae.

The sea otter (*Enhydra lutris*) is considered a

 keystone species in North Pacific kelp forests, similar to the role of the *Pisaster* starfish in the rocky intertidal zone. Otters eat a variety of prey including crabs, sea urchins, abalone, other mollusks and slow moving fish, up to nine kilograms/20 pounds of food per day. Amazingly, in a study in the Aleutian Islands, otters with a density of 20 to 30 animals per square kilometre/52 to 78 animals per square mile consumed about 35,000 kilograms/77,000 pounds of prey annually. However, the relationship of the otter and one of its prey items, the sea urchin that regulates kelp forest distribution.

Sea urchins in the genus *Stronglyocentrotus* graze directly on kelp beds and often eat through the holdfast anchoring the algae to the bottom. Detached kelp is then swept away by ocean currents. Otters eat sea urchins and this maintains urchin density, protecting the kelp from over-grazing. At one point it was thought the American lobster (*Homerus americanus*) performed a similar keystone function in western Atlantic kelp forests. However, further research found that kelp and urchin fluctuations are more likely natural events triggered by environmental variation. Although questions remain, it's clear that urchin density regulates kelp community ecology.

POLAR REGIONS

© Michel Verdure

Primary productivity in polar seas nothing short of massive, mostly due to the lack of thermal stratification that would prevent the recycling of nutrients through upwelling. But, this productivity is highly seasonal and mainly confined to the summer's 24-hour days. During these times, ample nutrients and sunlight result in spectacular plankton blooms. However, this short-lived summer productivity peak doesn't compensate for the long and unproductive winter months. The Arctic Ocean's productivity in the Northern Hemisphere is limited by landmasses that interrupt water circulation and upwelling. In the southern ocean around Antarctica, water movement is not restricted and upwelling replaces the cold, dense water, which sinks near the continent. The rich

© Amos Nachoum

mixture is stirred by the Antarctic Circumpolar current and accounts for a much greater share of high latitude primary productivity than the Arctic.

The Southern Polar Ocean

The Southern Ocean is interesting because it make up nearly a quarter of the world ocean but contains one-tenth of its heat, averaging a bone chilling 2° C/36° F. During the winter, approximately 20 million square kilometres/8 million square miles of the Antarctic Ocean are covered by ice. Because this ice cover modifies heat and moisture exchange between the ocean and atmosphere, any change in ice cover will likely affect the region's oceanic and atmospheric

THE GREENHOUSE EFFECT AND SEA LEVEL RISE

Is it getting warmer out? Even if it's winter, the answer is yes. Global temperatures have been steadily increasing over the last 18,000 years, but it is only in the last several centuries that the rate of this temperature rise has increased. Many scientists feel that this acceleration in world temperature is due to the *greenhouse effect*. Since the Industrial Revolution, humans have been producing more and more carbon dioxide. This carbon dioxide is released in the atmosphere and acts as a heat blanket. As with a greenhouse, solar radiation penetrates to the earth's surface, but heat that would normally radiate out and away from the planet are trapped by greenhouse gasses, such as carbon dioxide, chlorofluorocarbons (CFCs) and methane.

So what does this all mean for the world ocean? Although climate is one of the most difficult natural processes to predict, the effect on the marine environment is potentially damaging. If warming partially melts glacial ice, this could add significantly to the ocean's volume, causing its level to rise. Low-lying, coastal, island and other areas could be inundated and perhaps disappear. Given the trend of increasing coastal populations, this is a potential problem. In addition, a rapid increase in sea level might outpace coral growths and interrupt the nutrient circulation necessary for productive food webs.

It is important to note the uncertainty in any climate prediction, especially one that is so complex and dependent upon so many variables. One prospect for the future is to decrease the reliance on fossil fuels. Although this in itself is a contentious issue (using nuclear fuel as an alternative, for example), finding an economically viable alternative fuel source provides the best hope for a reduction in greenhouse gas production.

© Michel Verdure

circulation patterns.

The Earth's surface temperature has been rising for the last 100 years and this rise is causing concern about its effect on the Antarctic ice sheet. If a small portion of the Antarctic ice sheet melts, global sea level could rise. However, some researchers feel increasing snowfall might actually thicken the sheet and lower sea level.

Perhaps even more concerning is the growing hole in the protective ozone layer above the Antarctic. Ozone is a highly reactive oxygen molecule that forms a layer in the upper atmosphere shielding life on Earth from potentially damaging solar radiation. Chlorofluorocarbons (CFCs) are widely used chemicals that react with ozone and deplete the ozone layer. This degradation of the ozone layer allows increased levels of ultraviolet radiation to reach the Earth's surface. This radiation from the Sun could be particularly detrimental to land plants, phytoplankton and kelp that form the base of the food chain.

Antarctica is a peculiar place. Although it is actually the world's largest desert, receiving only five centimetres/two inches of precipitation annually, its ice cap contains up to 80 percent of the earth's fresh water. Moving offshore, Antarctica's continental shelf drops off to 600 metres/2000 feet, as opposed to the average 150 metres/500 feet found off most continents. This extreme depth results from the tremendous weight of the continent itself and its ice cap, which force the continent down into the semi-solid mantle of the earth.

Some of the Antarctic's water is also different than that found off most other continents. Antarctic Bottom Water is the densest of any ocean water and is formed as seawater freezes near the continent. When water freezes and crystallizes, salts are excluded to form brine. This dense water then sinks and spreads across the seabed, sometimes even taking more than a thousand years to creep into the Northern Hemisphere. Although it moves slowly, Antarctic Bottom Water forms quickly, with 20 to 50 million cubic metres/26 to 65 million cubic yards formed every second.

Not surprisingly, the Antarctic is very cold and has the honor of the lowest temperature in recorded history. In 1983, scientists logged an official reading of -89.2° C/-128.6° F. Because it is so cold and there is no food available on the continent, resident bird and mammal populations must take to the sea for survival. In fact, only the Emperor penguin (*Aptenodytes forsteri*) winters in Antarctica.

Although the terrestrial environment lacks natural resources, this is not the case in the marine environment. A thumb-sized crustacean called krill (*Euphausia superba*) is the key to this ecosystem. During the short summer, herbivorous krill consume phytoplankton during the summer bloom. Seabirds, squid, fishes and even whales then eat tremendous amounts of krill. The Antarctic Ocean produces from 500 to 750 million metric tons/551 to 827 million tons of Krill each year, with the greatest concentrations in the Weddell Sea's upwelling currents. And, although they're considered zooplankton, krill act more like schooling fish and move horizontally rather than vertically as do most other plankton. A research team tracked once tracked a "school" of krill across 278 kilometres/172 miles over 14 days.

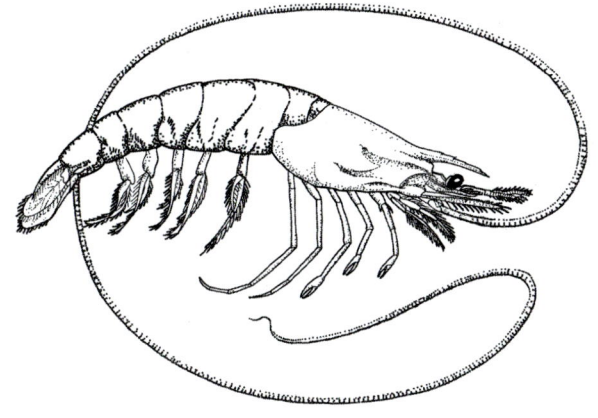

Krill (Euphausia superba)

The Antarctic region contains significant mineral and biological resources but lacked, until recently, any international agreement concerning resource use. The Antarctic's living marine resources, particularly whale species, have long histories of over-exploitation. Hunting pressure on the right whale (*Balaena glacialis*) and sperm whale (*Physeter catodon*) subsided in the 19th century when substitute products

became available, but modern ships and explosive-tipped harpoons threaten the blue whale (*Balaenoptera musculus*) and fin whale (*Balaenopteraphysalus*). In the 1930's, 43,000 whales were killed during one season alone. Today, populations are only one-sixth to one-tenth of their pre-hunting numbers. For example, Antarctic blue whales were once a quarter million strong, but now number less than 500. Humpback whales are in a similar position, now numbering in the thousands.

Today, international agreement has led to better management of the Antarctic's resources. The Antarctic Treaty was ratified in 1961 by twelve countries and prohibited military activities on the continent, promoted scientific cooperation and set aside territorial sovereignty disputes. Since that time, forty-four countries have signed on to the treaty, which remains in effect indefinitely. However, the original provisions of the treaty have been strengthened through five additional international agreements. These are the Agreed Measures for the Conservation of Antarctic Fauna and Flora, the Convention for the Conservation of Antarctic Seals, the Convention on the Conservation of Antarctic Marine Living Resources, the Convention on the Regulation of Antarctic Mineral Resource Activities and the Protocol on Environmental Protection to the Antarctic Treaty. These agreements are collectively known as the Antarctic Treaty System and aim to protect the continent as much as possible.

The Northern Polar Ocean

While Antarctica is a continent surrounded by ocean, the Arctic is an ocean surrounded by continents. Capped with a layer of pack ice that averages three metres/10 feet thick, wind and expansion can force the ice into ridges pushing up to 10 metres/33 feet above sea level and more than 40 metres/130 feet below. The earth's widest continental shelves lie beneath the Arctic Ocean and harbor some of the coldest water in the sea. Arctic waters are also less saline than those of the Antarctic due to the summer freshwater input from Siberian and Canadian rivers.

Arctic Ocean circulation differs greatly from that of the Antarctic because there is no northern equivalent to the Antarctic Circumpolar Current. Unlike most others ocean bodies, the Arctic Ocean is virtually surrounded by Greenland, Eurasia and North America and more than 80 percent of its water movement occurs in the Greenland Sea, a narrow gap between Greenland and Spitzbergen Island. This is the Arctic's only deep-water connection to the world ocean. A smaller portion—less than 20 percent—flows through the shallow

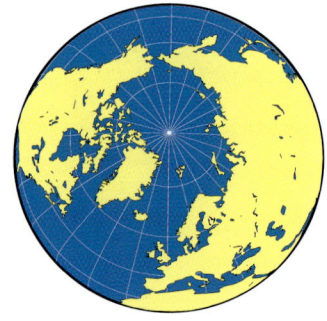

The Arctic

Bering Straits into the Pacific.

Because the region has more open water, the Arctic isn't quite as inhospitable as the Antarctic and the ice packs support more large animals than in the Southern Hemisphere. Winds and currents create openings in the pack ice, called polynyas, which some seals and whales use as breathing holes, while polar bears (*Ursus maritimus*) and killer whales (*Orcinus orca*) come to prey on seals. As a result, some seals and even the polar bear have been spotted as far north as the pole. The pack ice is also a temporary home for a few bird species, one species of hare and sometimes even humans.

Two percent of the water from the Arctic Ocean travels as icebergs. They *calve*, or break, from the Greenland ice cap and flow in the Labrador Current between Greenland and Baffin Island into the Atlantic. Unlike the flat icebergs that form in the Antarctic, icebergs in the Arctic are more mountainous and are called glacier-type.

© NOAA/Department of Commerce

The Arctic region has some important resources, including several fisheries and significant oil and gas deposits. But, as with Antarctica, primary productivity in the Arctic is seasonal because little to no photosynthesis occurs during the winter, resulting in a total productivity one-tenth of that in temperate seas.

Commercial fur seal hunting has occurred in the Arctic since the 16th century, but has halted in the recent past. Although commercial hunting has stopped, indigenous peoples of North America, Siberia and Greenland continue subsistence hunting. This minimal take appears to have no discernable effect on the whale populations in the region.

QUIZ

1. The ocean's main source of primary productivity is:
   a. deep-sea hydrothermal vents
   b. the aphotic zones
   c. phytoplankton
   d. coral reefs
2. True or False. A plankton bloom is a peak in productivity, usually in the spring.
3. Intertidal organisms face which of the following threats? (choose all that apply)
   a. wave action
   b. desiccation
   c. predation
   d. all of the above
4. True or False. Zonation is the grouping of distinct plants and animals in the intertidal.
5. Zonation of rocky intertidal organisms depends on which of the following factors? (choose all that apply)
   a. tidal levels.
   b. physical factors.
   c. biological factors.
   d. density of periwinkle per square metre/square foot.
6. True or False. Kelps are vascular plants that are not important as habitat for marine organisms.
7. An organism that effects the ecosystem disproportionately to its numbers or density is called a:
   a. mollusk
   b. barnacle
   c. keystone species
   d. all of the above
8. True or False. The key to Antarctica's productive food web is the herbivorous crustacean krill.
9. The Arctic supports more large animals than the Antarctic because:
   a. it has a greater landmass.
   b. the amount of open water results in lower temperature.
   c. its waters are less dense than those in the Antarctic.
   d. the Arctic's proximity to Greenland.

How did you do? 1. c; 2. True 3. d; 4. True 5. a, b and c 6. False – kelp is an algae and kelp forests are home to a diverse community of animals; 7. c; 8. True; 9. c.

CHAPTER FOUR
CORAL REEFS—
RAINFORESTS OF THE SEA

CORAL REEFS—
RAINFORESTS OF THE SEA

- **CORAL REEFS—
  DIVERSITY AND BEAUTY**
- **REEF FISH**
- **LIMITS TO ABUNDANCE**
- **THREATS—
  NATURAL AND HUMAN-INDUCED**

STUDY QUESTIONS
Underline/highlight the answers
to these questions as you read:
1. Why are coral reefs so important to the marine environment?
2. Why is the term *biotic reef* more accurate than *coral reef*?
3. Approximately how many different species of fish exist on coral reefs?
4. What percentage of the world's coral reefs are threatened, and how is this threat likely to continue in the future?
5. What are the natural and human-induced factors currently contributing to the destruction of coral reefs?
6. What is the estimated effect of recreational diving on coral reef destruction?

CORAL REEFS—
DIVERSITY AND BEAUTY

"In the scope of the endangered ecosystem, the coral reef environment is a precious resource we, as divers, hold close to our hearts. And, we are fortunate that we, as individuals, have the power to protect it."

– Drew Richardson, Senior Vice President, PADI
Vice President, Project AWARE Foundation

Coral Reefs—Diversity and Beauty

There's no more special place on earth to those who dive or snorkel than a coral reef. Temperate areas offer thrilling sights and great places to dive (see Chapter 3), but most divers also look forward to visiting spectacular tropical coral gardens to watch their colorful inhabitants. This makes coral reef health of particular concern to underwater explorers.

Beyond their innate beauty and popularity as dive and snorkel sites, coral reefs are habitat and nursery grounds for 25 percent of all known marine species – many of which humans rely on for food. This is an impressive statistic considering how little of the sea bottom is coral reef. While the total range is difficult to determine, the most accepted figure is that coral reefs cover only about 600,000 square kilometres/230,000 square miles. That's about one-tenth of one percent of the total sea bottom, or an area about the size of the province of British Columbia or the nation of Venezuela.

Coral reefs are important because they are storehouses of biodiversity. The term *coral reef* does not do justice to the complexity of these ecosystems. They could more accurately be called *biotic reefs*. Some biologists refer to reefs as *rainforests of the oceans* because they support an incredible array of organisms. Pharmacologists have found an abundance of biomedical compounds on reefs, from antibiotics to anti-cancer agents, and suspect there are thousands more yet to be discovered.

From a purely physical perspective, coral reefs are vital structures. They protect islands and coastal communities from storms, wave damage and erosion. The Coral Reef Alliance (CORAL) estimates that each square metre/yard of coral reef protects about $47,000 US in property values.

Many tropical nations base their tourism industries on the appeal of the surrounding coral reefs. In some areas, reef diving or snorkeling tours are significant income sources and are foundational to the countries' economies.

The Coral

© Michel Verdure

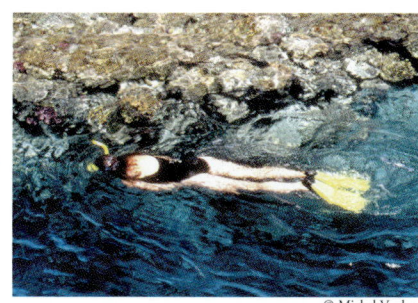

Corals grow best in the shallow, clear water of tropical and subtropical oceans where the annual temperature range is between 18-30° C/64-86° F. Reefs are actually massive coral colonies. Corals are tiny marine invertebrates (from the phylum Cnidaria) that secrete skeletons of calcium carbonate

© Michel Verdure

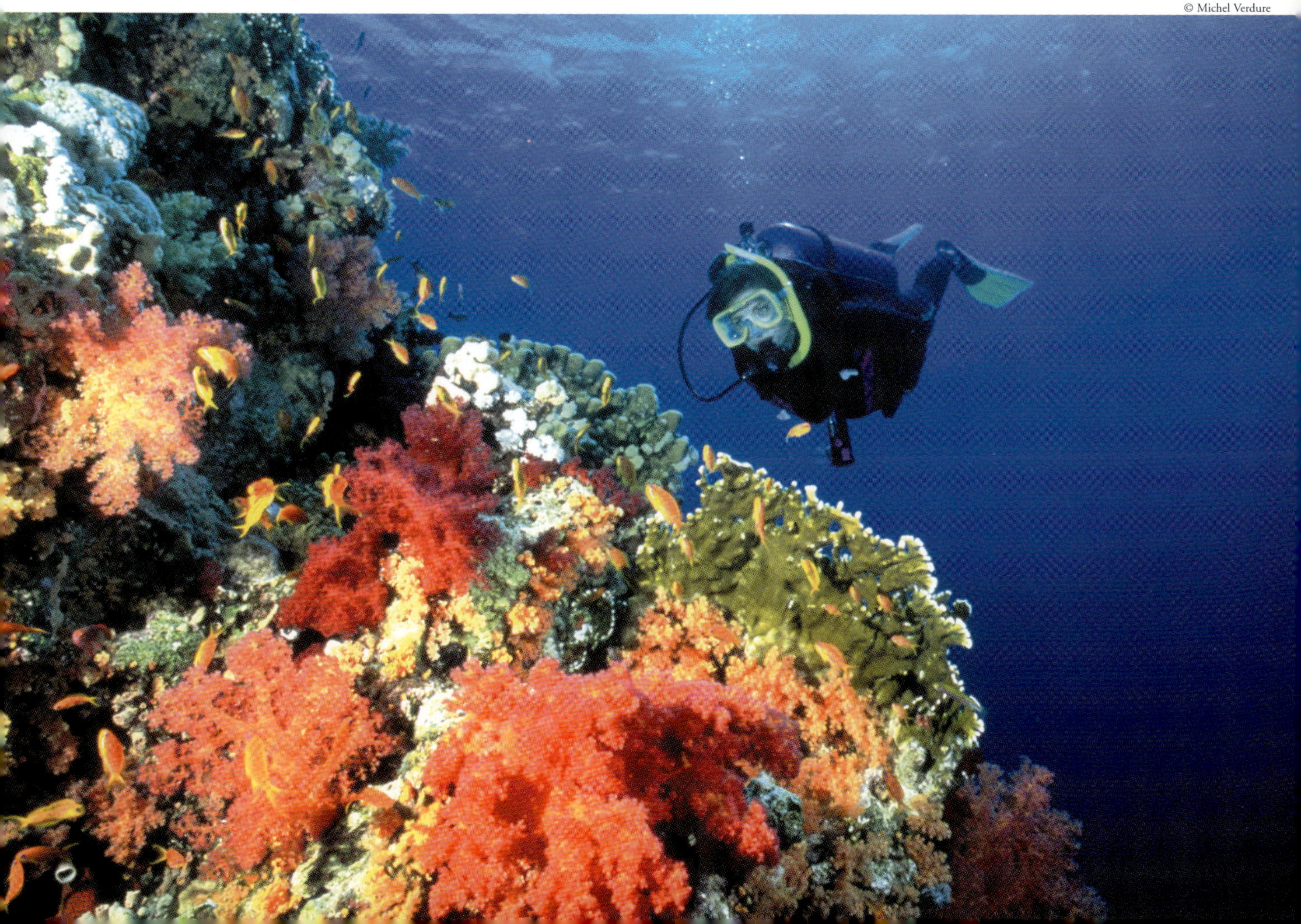

Photo by Tom Haight

(limestone) to form small cups called corallites. The reef grows as individual coral animals, called polyps, that anchor within these limestone cups to collectively form large structures.

Most corals are impressive builders. The largest structure on earth manufactured by living organisms is Australia's Great Barrier Reef, which is visible even from outer space.

Corals that build massive reefs (*hermatypic* or mound building corals) have a special symbiotic relationship with the algae that reside deep within the polyp's tissues. This algae (*zooxanthellae*) enables a coral colony to function as both plant and animal. The algae produces food via photosynthesis, while the polyp catches plankton from the water column. The algae releases oxygen and sugars that are consumed by the polyp and the coral releases carbon dioxide and nitrogenous waste that sustain the algae. Because algae depend on light, reef-building corals do not grow well deeper than 25 metres/82 feet.

When a coral colony dies, either through natural or human-induced factors, it forms a substrate on which new corals grow. Coralline algae (algae that itself secretes limestone) cements the sand and coral fragments together to fill in the spaces between the larger fragments of dead coral skeletons. This cementing process and growth provides stability and makes reefs less susceptible to damage from waves and storms.

The Reef

Coral may form a reef's foundation, but reef ecosystems flourish due to an amazing menagerie of other organisms. For example, bacteria and algae coat the sandy bottom and portions of the reef not covered by living coral. This provides food for mollusks, crustaceans, sea cucumbers, sea urchins

Photo by Robert Baker

> **SAME SLOW GROWTH RATE?**
> Contrary to popular belief, all corals do not grow at the same rate. In fact, there are considerable differences among species. For example, branching corals like staghorn coral can grow horizontally about 10 centimetres/four inches per year, while massive forms like boulder coral grow at one-tenth this rate. Vertical growth differs as well and can be as slow as less than a few millimetres/fractions of an inch per year in the Red Sea.

and herbivorous fish. These organisms, in turn, provide vital housekeeping functions that keep the ecosystem healthy and also serve as food sources for organisms higher up on the food chain.

Other organisms, such as sponges, worms and mollusks, play an important role by eroding a reef's massive limestone fortresses. This type of erosion is a positive force because it creates additional living space within the reef. Scientists estimate that as much as 40 percent of a coral reef is actually open space. Broken segments of coral provide new habitats and are eventually cemented back into the reef by coralline algae. The actions of grazers such as parrotfish and sea urchins produce large quantities of sediment, which also results in new living spaces for smaller fish and invertebrates.

REEF FISH

Photo by Katherine Smith

There are more than 21,000 species of fish worldwide, with more than 4000 species found on coral reefs. Many reef fish display vibrant colors arranged in intriguing patterns, while others have a single hue or features that allow them to blend in with their surroundings. Reef fish are generally small in comparison to fish that inhabit the open ocean, yet their sizes and shapes vary widely.

Their behavior, food sources, reproduction strategies, life cycles and survival techniques also differ considerably. For example, damselfish dart about in almost constant motion, while scorpionfish lie quietly, camouflaged from unsuspecting prey. Parrotfish sleep under ledges sometimes protected by a mucous cocoon, while cardinalfish come out from hiding at night. Also, most butterflyfish mate for life, while male hawkfish tend to gather harems.

Identifying Fish

Because there are so many different reef fish species, it is impossible to learn all of them or even most of them. However, the most commonly encountered fish tend to belong to the same few families (30 to 50), which makes general identification a little easier.

Project AWARE Foundation, PADI and Reef Environmental Education Foundation (REEF) jointly developed the PADI Specialty Diver course AWARE - Fish Identification that emphasizes fish watching by identifying common characteristics among fish families rather than individual species. Through training materials obtained from REEF or other available sources, students learn the key characteristics of fish families and identify them by placing them in groups. The 12 commonly used groups that include more than 30 different fish families are:

1. Butterflyfish, angelfish and surgeonfish - This group usually have thin bodies and are oval or disk shaped.  They are also generally bright and have interesting patterns. Most Butterflyfish are round with small bodies and concave foreheads. They also have elongated mouths to pick tiny invertebrates from crevices. Angelfish have long dorsal fins and rounded foreheads. Surgeonfish are also called tangs and are usually a solid color and have spines protruding from each side of the base of the tail.

2. Jacks, barracuda, porgy and chubs - This group is usually silver in color with forked tails. They are also some of the larger fish on the reef. Jacks, also called trevally, are open water silver and blue fish. These large fish are strong swimming predators. Barracudas are distinct fish with long cylindrical  silver bodies and large mouths with sharp teeth. Porgies, which are also called sea bream, are usually oval shaped with steep sloping heads. Chubs, or rudderfish, have elongated oval shaped bodies and are usually silver and found higher in the water column.

3. Snappers and grunts - These fish have long tapered bodies with heads that slope down to their mouths. Snappers have upturned mouths with visible canine teeth.  Grunts, so named because of the noise they make, they are colorful and often congregate in groups. They are also known as sweetlips.

4. Damselfish, chromis and hamlets - These small oval fish are often seen darting in and out of crevices. The are often colorful and display many different patterns and shadings. Damselfish are algae-eaters that defend their territory, even charging divers to protect their nest.  Chromis are have bodies that are more elongated

than damselfish and have deeply forked tails. Hamlets are actually members of the seabass family but are shaped similar to damselfish with flatter sloping heads.

5. Groupers, seabass and basslets - Grouper is the common name for the larger seabass family members. Usually big-bodied with large mouths and lips, grouper are some of the larger fish seen on reefs and are often in the shadows by themselves. They also have a short, spiny dorsal fin that softens as it tapers down the tail. The other members of the seabass family are smaller and have more elongated bodies than grouper. Basslets are tiny, colorful fish that usually inhabit deeper reefs or walls.

6. Parrotfish and wrasses - Usually colorful, this group includes parrotfish with their beak-like teeth plates and rainbow colors, while wrasse are generally smaller and have elongated bodies. Parrotfish use their bony beaks to scrape algae off of hard surfaces. Wrasses forage for small invertebrates in the sand.

© Michel Verdure

7. Squirrelfish, bigeyes and cardinalfish - This group is primarily nocturnal, ranging over the reef freely at night but hiding in cracks and crevices during the day. You can spot them by looking for their reddish color and big eyes. Squirrelfish have a pronounced rear dorsal fin that resembles a squirrel's tail. Bigeyes have a continuous dorsal fin, large eyes and are less scaly. Cardinalfish are small reddish fish with short snouts and two separate dorsal fins.

8. Blennies, gobies and jawfish - These small fish with long bodes are often found on the bottom backed into small holes with only their head poking out. Blennies will perch themselves up on their pectoral fins and are distinguished by the appendages on their head, called cirri, that appear to be eyebrows or little horns. Gobies rest on their pectoral fins in a straight, flat and motionless position and are referred to as a cleaner fish. Jawfish have long bodies and large jaws and are often found in holes constructed by moving stones.

Photo by Michael Boyer

9. Flounders, scorpionfish, lizardfish and frogfish - These bottom dwellers demonstrate excellent camouflage and unusual shapes. Flounders are a flatfish with both eyes on the side which faces the surface. They also often burrow into the sand. Scorpionfish are camouflaged to match their

surroundings and have stocky bodies and spiny venomous dorsal fins. Lizardfish have elongated bodies with large upturned mouths and rest on the bottom. Frogfish, also called anglerfish, have bulky bodies, webbed pectoral and ventral fins and large upturned mouths. They attract small fish by dangling a wiry appendage in front of their mouth to act as bait.

10. Filefish, triggerfish, puffers, trunkfish, cowfish, goatfish, trumpetfish and drums - This group is made up of all unusually shaped free-swimming fish. Filefish and triggerfish comprise a family of fish called leatherjackets because of their tough skin. They have thin bodies and distinctive prominent lips. Puffers have the ability to draw water into their bodies to inflate their size. Some of these have spines which are erect when the fish expands. Trunkfish and cowfish are called boxfish due to their triangular shape and bony scales. Goatfish are long and cylindrical and have distinctive barbells that hang down from their chin. Trumpetfish have tubelike bodies and long mouths that flair open to suck in prey. Drums have extremely long

foredorsal fin and striking black and while coloration.

11. Eels - These fish have long snakelike bodies and spend the day in crevices, holes or under ledges.

They are found free swimming mostly at night.

12. Sharks and rays - These fish have an internal "skeleton" made of cartilage. Sharks use their tails for

propulsion while rays have modified pectoral fins that they use to swim in a flying motion.

Limits to Abundance

In biology, the term *gross primary production* (GPP) describes the total amount of living matter in a given area produced by plants. It's a way of quantifying the base of the food chain. In nutrient-rich coastal areas, the GPP is high and in the open ocean the GPP is very low. Logically, coral reefs should rank in between, but lower on the scale. However, they often have a GPP that is 250 times more than the surrounding ocean. This makes reefs one of the highest production areas of any natural ecosystem.

This seeming violation of the laws of thermodynamics — high productivity in nutrient poor water — is quite complex and not completely understood. But, in general, this occurs because corals and coral communities are extremely efficient at recycling nutrients (nitrate and phosphate). The nutrients that make their way there tend to stay there.

From their high GPP, it seems reasonable to assume that coral reefs produce far more food than is needed by inhabitants, however reef production is nearly balanced by what it consumes – there is little surplus. This balance has important implications for coral reef fisheries. Unlike productive ocean ecosystems, the amount of organic matter (fish and invertebrates) that can be taken without causing damage to the coral community is limited. A coral reef that has adequately supported a limited sustenance fishery for centuries would likely collapse within a matter of years once commercial fishing was introduced.

What is REEF and how can you get involved?

REEF (Reef Environmental Education Foundation) is a private, nonprofit organization established in 1990 by underwater photographers and marine life authors Paul Humann and Ned DeLoach. REEF's mission is to educate, enlist and enable divers and nondivers to become active participants in conserving marine habitats. One way REEF carries out its mission is by providing vital reef and inshore fish biodiversity data to marine scientists, resource managers, conservationists and other interested parties by enlisting and mobilizing volunteer recreational divers and snorkelers to conduct underwater surveys.

Through REEF's program, fish watching becomes more than merely an enjoyable activity — you can personally contribute to the understanding and conservation of the aquatic environment. The REEF Fish Survey Project is an ongoing cooperative effort between REEF and The Nature Conservancy (TNC). TNC is a private, nonprofit organization established in 1951 to preserve plants, animals and natural communities that represent the diversity of life on earth by protecting the lands and waters they need to survive.

Through the Project, volunteers gather large amounts of species and abundance data, which is transferred into the Project database. The database provides the scientific, resource management and conservation communities with access to long-term and geographically broad species inventories, as well as historical records of reef fish populations.

To participate in the REEF Fish Survey Project, you need basic fish identification skills and must be a member of REEF. PADI's AWARE Fish Identification Specialty course is a great way to develop these skills. Developed by Project AWARE in conjunction with REEF, the specialty course introduces divers to the most common families and species of fish found in the diver's local area and teaches fish surveying so you can participate in the REEF Fish Survey Project.

THREATS—NATURAL AND HUMAN-INDUCED

In a widely quoted address to the 7th International Coral Reef Symposium, Dr. Clive Wilkinson of the Australian Institute of Marine Science made the dire observation that perhaps as much as 10 percent of the world's coral reefs are already degraded beyond recovery; another 30 percent are likely to die within the next 10-20 years, and still another 30 percent could die 20-40 years thereafter. That means 70 percent of the world's coral reefs may be dead by the middle of this century.

A survey by the International Union for the Conservation of Nature and Natural Resources (IUCN), also known as the World Conservation Union, found that human activities have significantly damaged or destroyed reefs in 93 of the 109 countries where they occur. The reefs at greatest risk are in South and Southeast Asia, east Africa and the Caribbean.

Will coral reefs survive for future generations? Unfortunately, we don't know. However, one thing is certain — the only possible way for coral reefs to survive is to protect them politically. Affected nations need to develop and promote environmental programs that strongly discourage destruction and make conservation appealing to fisheries and industry.

Reef Sensitivity

Coral reefs are threatened by both human and natural causes. They are susceptible because they live within a very narrow tolerance range in respect to light, temperature and nutrition. If the water is too warm or too cool, corals can die of thermal stress. If the water gets too turbid and blocks light, they may suffer from starvation due to reduced photosynthesis. Nutrient-laden water may cause corals to be out-competed

Coral Reef Exposed to Air During Low Tide
Photo by Anthony Ellis

and overgrown by nutrient-loving macroalgae. Quick sea level shifts may leave a reef too deep or too shallow to adjust and cause its slow death.

Because of coral's sensitivity to even the slightest change in environmental conditions, reefs are one of the first ecosystems affected by pollution or atmospheric alterations. Many scientists from different disciplines study these fragile communities for early warning signs of environmental degradation and global climate change. Acting as ecological indicators is another important coral reef function.

Coral Predator: The Crown of Thorns Sea Star (Acanthaster planci)
Photo by Brigit Jager

Natural Threats

Because coral reefs have been around for hundreds of millions of years, they can adapt to some change. Natural environmental conditions may damage reefs, but, provided nothing else adds to the stress, they can recover. In fact, the pressure placed on reefs by natural stresses may help them

NATURAL OR NOT?

Throughout the 1980s, large portions of normally colorful corals, sea whips and sponges on reefs worldwide turned white and died – a phenomenon called *coral bleaching*. Marine biologists noted bleaching in the Caribbean, Society Islands, Great Barrier Reef, Western Indian Ocean and Indonesia.

Most scientists agree that bleaching events are probably caused by many factors – some natural, such as El Niño, and others human-induced. Although it's controversial and not proven, some researchers claim that human-induced climate change is the primary culprit. Others believe that deteriorating water quality from pollution and storm runoff may make coral reefs more susceptible to disease and bleaching. The Biodiversity and Climate Change Programme at the United Nations Environment Programme World Conservation Monitoring Centre is currently studying the potential relationship between coral reef bleaching and human population density.

Coral Bleaching
© Reef Relief

evolve a high level of biodiversity. Threats from nature include:
- Global weather anomalies such as El Niño
- Severe storms (hurricanes, typhoons, etc.)
- Fresh water inundation
- Species blooms
- Exposure to air during extremely low tides
- Diseases

Human-induced Threats

Not surprisingly, the most severe threat to coral reefs is from human-induced changes to the environment. Many scientists and resource managers believe most of these occur on land. These threats include increasing population pressure and technology-enhanced coastal development. Unlike pre-industrial societies that had minimal effects on coastal environments, today's heavy machinery, mechanical dredges and other industrial building innovations easily transform coastal zones into cities and resort communities with little regard for their effects on nearby reefs.

Deforestation, overgrazing and poor land-use practices lead to massive soil erosion and river siltation. Sediment dumped onto coral reefs blocks out light, while domestic, agricultural and industrial waste such as fertilizers, pesticides and sewage from development brings an overabundance of nutrients. The result is that corals die and once-healthy reefs take on a drab appearance.

Resource abuse offshore, such as overfishing and coral mining, can also have devastating effects on reefs. Indicators of overfishing, such as decreases in average and maximum sizes as well as changes in the variety of fish caught, often go unrecognized because of poor fisheries management. Dwindling catches cause fishers to turn to more destructive practices like dynamiting and cyanide poisoning. Overfishing may remove the reef cleaners and algae grazers, which allows algae to out-compete the corals.

In Southeast Asia, destructive industries — such as coral harvesting for building materials and souvenirs have devastated large reef tracts and brought species like the giant *Tridacna* clam to the brink of extinction. Even the aquarium trade has had an effect on populations of fish, invertebrates and "live rock", or reef, removed from the environment.

A final, steadily growing threat to coral reefs is the effect of tourism. Although tourism can be an environmentally friendly way to generate income from coral reefs, this

A Reef with Dead Coral

Photo by Claire Ellis

happens only when resort development and operations are carefully controlled. Certainly, some damage occurs to reefs from activities such as sport fishing, anchoring and accidental contact by snorkelers and divers. However, in most cases, these activities cause relatively minor damage in comparison to other threats. And most certainly, divers and snorkelers or marine tourists are uniquely positioned to further minimize their minor damage by interacting responsibly with the marine environment. Anchor damage is one activity that can be curtailed completely through the use of mooring buoys. A mooring buoy is a permanent anchor line to which a boat can attach over a dive or fishing site, precluding any potential anchor damage to reefs. Project AWARE supports the installation and use of mooring buoys and has compiled an extensive mooring buoy planning guide outlining the components that need to be considered when taking on such a project.

The bigger culprit is untreated sewage and other wastes from tourist facilities that pollute reef areas. Also, immediate damage occurs when builders situate resorts in coastal habitats like beaches, mangrove forests and seagrass beds.

Perhaps the most poorly understood human-induced threat involves changes to the atmosphere. Though still controversial, a growing number of scientists believe ozone depletion and increases in greenhouse gases could have serious consequences for coral reef health. Ozone depletion permits the passage of greater quantities of potentially damaging ultraviolet radiation. Data indicates this increase is highly destructive to corals and other zooxanthellae-hosting organisms.

Photo by Anthony Ellis

Global climate changes wreak havoc in several ways, including raising sea surface temperature, altering the pattern, distribution and frequency of tropical storms, changing rainfall patterns and causing variations in ocean currents.

Summary of Human-induced Reef Stresses
- Coastal area overpopulation
- Coastal area development for ports, homes and resorts
- Siltation from inland erosion, especially in areas near large rivers and estuaries
- Pollution and eutrophication from chemicals, fertilizers, pesticides and sewage
- Overfishing resulting in disruption of ecological balance
- Destructive fishing methods, such as the use of dynamite and cyanide
- Extracting coral and coral sand for construction materials and souvenirs
- Removing fish and invertebrates, including live rock, for the aquarium trade
- Excessive collection of corals, shells, fish and other reef organisms
- Anchor and collision damage
- Atmospheric alteration

Project AWARE's Coral Reef Conservation Initiative

With the proliferation of natural and human-induced threats to coral reef habitats, Project AWARE has addressed these problems head-on with the coral reef conservation initiative. Built on the successful model of the Protect the Sharks campaign, this informational campaign is designed to raise public awareness through informational brochures, display posters, stickers and other campaign materials, plus organize and actively participate in various conferences and legislative efforts. The initiative will also include heavy media attention through articles in dive publications, press conferences and public service announcements.

In addition to the public awareness campaign, Project AWARE's coral reef conservation initiative includes an educational program that features a PADI Specialty course and training for resource managers. This specialty course consists of a classroom module and a practical application (dive)

module developed in association with the conservation organization Oceanwatch. Each portion of the course stands alone, but can be combined for the full certification. This worldwide campaign raises awareness and provides an outlet for divers and ocean-lovers to contribute to the preservation of coral reef habitats.

Quiz

1. Coral reefs are important to the marine environment because they:
   a. are nursery grounds for 25 percent of all known marine species.
   b. are storehouses for biodiversity.
   c. act as barriers to protect island lagoons and coastal areas.
   d. All of the above are correct.
2. True or False. Some biologists refer to coral reefs as *rainforests of the ocean* because they support a biologically diverse array of organisms.
3. Of the approximately 21,000 species of fish worldwide, more than _____ species are found on coral reefs.
   a. 16,000   c. 4000
   b. 8000   d. 2000
4. True or False. Today, as much as 50 percent of the world's coral reefs may be degraded beyond recovery.
5. Which of the following are human-induced threats to coral reefs? (choose all that apply)
   a. Fresh water inundation.
   b. Using cyanide and dynamite to catch fish.
   c. Siltation that results from coastal construction.
   d. Anchor damage.
6. True or False. Accidental contact by snorkelers and divers causes relatively minor damage to coral reefs.

How did you do? 1. d; 2. True 3. c; 4. False – estimates are closer to 10 percent 5. b, c and d 6. True

CHAPTER FIVE
AQUATIC RESOURCES IN PERIL

POLLUTION

AQUATIC RESOURCES IN PERIL

- **POLLUTION**
- **FISHERIES CONCERNS**
- **COASTAL ZONE AND WETLAND DEGRADATION**

STUDY QUESTIONS

Underline/highlight the answers to these questions as you read:
1. What are the sources of pollution entering the aquatic environment?
2. What is the largest source of oil pollution, and what are some of the consequences of this pollution in the environment?
3. What effects do organic matter, solid wastes, discarded munitions, heat effluent, and the introduction of alien species have on the aquatic environment?
4. What is the *Tragedy of the Commons?*
5. Why are many marine fisheries near collapse?
6. What is *bycatch* and what effect does it have on marine ecosystems?
7. What are some of today's most destructive fishing practices?
8. How do world populations affect coastal zones?
9. What pressures contribute to the destruction of wetlands?

For all the life-sustaining resources our water provides, humans seem to return enormous amounts of waste and garbage. Each year, more than 20 billion metric tons/22 billion tons of pollutants are dumped into aquatic environments, primarily from land-based sources and atmospheric deposition. The ocean is the largest receptacle of direct dumping and pollution flowing in from large rivers. According to the United Nations Environmental Programme (UNEP), the amount and types of marine pollution can be attributed to the following:

- 44 percent – agricultural and industrial runoff.
- 33 percent – propellants, hydrocarbons (organic compounds like methane and benzene that contain only hydrogen and carbon) and biocides (substances such as antibiotics or pesticides that can kill other organisms).
- 12 percent – maritime accidents or ships dumping bilge water, ballast water and garbage.
- 10 percent – industrial, municipal or agricultural waste dumping and dredge spoil.

Once dumped in the sea or other aquatic environment, pollutants may not stay there. Through natural physical processes, some pollutants return to the atmosphere, dissolve or are ingested by organisms, whereas water movement and current may move pollution tremendous distances. For example, hydrocarbons detected in the waters surrounding Antarctica most likely originated thousands of kilometres/miles away.

Oil

For many, the word oil is synonymous with water pollution. Each year about 5.4 million metric tons/six million tons of petroleum hydrocarbons end up in the ocean and aquatic environments. Pollution sources include tanker and shipping operations and accidents, dry docking, offshore oil production, terminal loading, industrial and municipal waste, urban and river runoff, atmospheric fallout and natural seepage.

The most widely publicized episodes of oil pollution are tanker accidents, though such accidents account for only about five percent of oil entering the aquatic environment. Likewise, offshore drilling platforms can release oil into the sea, but the amount is even less than shipping-related causes. In total, oil transport and extraction activities account for little more than a quarter of the total ocean input. What is the primary cause of oil pollution? Oil users – *all* of us.

Most oil enters the aquatic environment from land-based sources such as runoff from parking lots (or other impervious surfaces) and effluent (waste material discharged into the

© Center for Marine Conservation

CLEANING IT UP

Various methods are used to deal with oil once it enters the aquatic environment:
- Chemical agents speed the emulsification of oil and disperse droplets so they don't reform as a slick.
- Chemically treated sand causes oil slicks to sink to the seabed.
- Chemical agents convert oil from a liquid to a gel so the slick can be rolled up like a carpet.
- Absorbents such as powdered cork, peat or straw are used to extract oil.
- Burning.

Ideally, oil should be treated before reaching shore where contamination becomes a much bigger problem. Beach cleaning is an enormous and costly job that often results in several other problems. Also, completely ridding a polluted site of oil takes a long time because bacteria and fungi must degrade the petroleum products.

environment) from wastewater treatment plants. An estimated 42 million litres/11 million gallons of oil per year, a quantity equal to the oil spilled in Alaska by the tanker *Exxon Valdez*, enters the oceans from the US alone. Wastewater treatment plants add more.

Another major culprit is our cars and trucks and our maintenance of them. Motor vehicle fuel burns incompletely and this releases petroleum hydrocarbons to the atmosphere which are then eventually washed to the sea by rain or snow. Along those same lines, often unwittingly, people changing the oil in their own vehicles discard the used oil down storm drains or other drainage areas. Since these areas, and storm drains in particular, empty directly into waterways untreated, this can contribute to oil pollution. In addition, in many cases this activity is illegal and simple to prevent by taking waste oil to a used oil collection center or recycling facility.

The final source of oil pollution is natural underground seepage. In fact, this natural source of pollution probably equals the amount of oil entering the ocean from atmospheric fallout and is twice that of tanker accidents.

The consequences of oil pollution are everywhere. Oil on a sea bird's plumage destroys its ability to repel water, causing it to become hypothermic or drown. In addition, relatively small quantities of ingested oil can depress egg laying and hatching success. Oil transferred from plumage to eggs can permeate the shells and kill the embryos.

Birds and marine mammals that swallow oil as they clean themselves may experience intestinal disorders or organ failure. Oil can kill many marine mammals, although there is no evidence that whales are at significant risk from oil pollution.

Even small concentrations of oil can taint entire fish or shellfish catches, rendering them unmarketable. Filter-feeders, such as clams and oysters, may take in tiny droplets of emulsified oil that are then incorporated into their tissues. This oil

© Ecoscene

gets passed up the food chain, causing damage and death long after the initial ingestion.

Manufactured Chemical Pollutants

More than 19 trillion litres/5 trillion gallons of toxic waste like heavy metals, halogenated hydrocarbons, industrial chemicals and radioactive substances enter the water each year. Many of these substances are not subject to bacterial decay and do not dissipate. These chemicals end up amassing in organisms – *bioaccumulation* – and become concentrated in predators further up the food chain until toxic levels are reached.

Chemicals or elements known to bioaccumulate include mercury, lead, copper, zinc and halogenated hydrocarbons. These substances can cause damage at any level of the food chain, though risks are greatest for top predators, like sharks and humans. These substances interfere with an organism's natural chemical processes. In aquatic organisms, even small doses may cause fin erosion, precancerous growths, skeletal deformities and abnormal larvae.

Hydrocarbons are organic chemicals containing hydrogen and carbon that combine with atoms of other elements, such as chlorine, fluorine, bromine or iodine, to form chlorinated hydrocarbons and halogenated hydrocarbons. Two chlorinated hydrocarbons are of note due to their hazardous nature in the aquatic environment, the pesticide dichloro-diphenyl-trichloroethane (DDT) and the industrial lubricants and coolants called polychlorinated biphenyls (PCBs).

DDT, once thought to be a safe and effective pesticide, was banned when it was linked to a large die-off of seabirds in the early 1960's. Over time, DDT would collect in the fatty tissue of seabird prey species. When the birds would consume enough contaminated fish, the DDT interfered with the calcium metabolism necessary for eggshell production. This resulted in thin and easily cracked eggshells and

© Ecoscene

the subsequent decline of many bird populations.

PCB contamination has resulted in marine organism death as far up the food chain as seals, sea lions and whales. In Canada's Saint Lawrence River, Beluga whales have accumulated high levels of halogenated hydrocarbons that contribute to digestive tract cancer from the benthic invertebrates they feed on. In the 1980's the population collapsed and necropsy performed on 72 animals revealed tumors, ulcers, respiratory ailments and failed immune systems related to PCBs.

Seawater is naturally radioactive, largely because of potassium and decay products from elements such as uranium and thorium. However, when we add radioactive substances by dumping waste, levels have the potential to become dangerous. Radioactive substances were released to the ocean during the 1940's because of nuclear weapons testing and radioactive solid waste disposal.

In 1975, the London Dumping Convention banned high-level radioactive waste dumping, but until then, significant amounts of radioactive waste made it to the sea. For

© NOAA/Department of Commerce

example, between 1946 and 1970, the United States dumped more than 110,000 barrels of plutonium and cesium waste into the ocean, often near densely populated areas.

Russia admitted that the former Soviet Union dumped both solid and liquid nuclear waste — including nuclear reactors — into its northern seas. In central Russia, Lake Karachay was a nuclear waste dumping ground for decades and now holds large quantities of radioactive waste.

A ban on low-level waste was added to the London Convention in 1983, but enforcement and safety concerns still remain. Radioactive material is often transported by ship and there's a risk of release if a shipping accident occurs.

Fortunately, marine organisms appear to have a relatively high tolerance to radioactivity and to date, there are no measurable environmental effects on ecosystems from existing levels of radiation in the sea. But who knows what the future holds?

Organic Matter

Organic matter actually contributes the greatest volume of waste to coastal waters. Because bacteria break down organic waste into inorganic products that enrich the marine ecosystem, a steady input is manageable and may be beneficial. However, if organic input exceeds its breakdown, this causes intense bacterial activity that depletes oxygen in the water.

Poorly oxygenated water favors plant life over animal life – a situation called *eutrophication* – which may result in dense phytoplankton blooms – red tides, as discussed in chapter 2. Red tides produce a neurotoxin that can be detrimental to other organisms in the area. Bivalves, such as oysters or clams, may accumulate toxins and pass them on to humans when eaten. This may result in illness or death.

Seafood contamination may also occur when organic matter containing human sewage reaches the water. Eating shellfish or fish with high amounts of accumulated human

CHEMICAL REACTIONS

There are now about 60,000 chemicals in use worldwide and each year the chemical industry introduces 200-1000 more. Every intentionally produced substance has an intended use and, unfortunately, many cause environmental problems. However, of greater concern are the unanticipated problems or unexpected adverse chemical reactions arising from new chemical development.

Chemical engineers use the phrase "indirect chemical end-products of supplementary chemical reactions" to describe these unforeseen consequences. The quantity, identity, and toxicity of many of these accidental end-products are often unknown.

To date, there are more than 3000 organic chemicals polluting the aquatic environment, and many of these substances show up in our drinking water. It is likely to be decades before we have irrefutable evidence concerning the effects of these organic micropollutants on our health.

© NOAA/Department of Commerce

pathogens can result in typhoid, salmonella poisoning, viral hepatitis and botulism. Dumping untreated or barely treated sewage causes serious public health concerns.

Solid Wastes

A major source of aquatic pollution is the *spoil* or soft bottom material dredged from ports, harbors, rivers and approach channels to keep them open to shipping. Dredge spoil often contains toxic chemicals, heavy metals and oil. While spoil is sometimes used as landfill, it's often dumped back in the water, thus redistributing the harmful substances.

Even when the spoil contains no hazardous materials, the spread of suspended particles clogs feeding and respiratory organs, reduces the light penetration needed for photosynthesis and smothers attached organisms when it finally settles. Disposing of any solid waste at sea is known to have negative effects on the natural communities inhabiting the dumping areas.

Plastics

The benefits of plastic — lightweight, strong and durable, not easily broken down — are also the drawbacks that make it such an environmental nightmare. Its hardiness makes it immune to natural decay mechanisms and microbial actions. For example, a plastic six-pack holder has a lifespan of 450 years in the average outdoor environment.

According to the Center for Marine Conservation (CMC), more than half of all marine debris is plastic. Common objects include fishing gear, plastic bags, packing materials, balloons, bottles and syringes. There is no place on earth — from remote Pacific atolls to Antarctica — that is spared the unsightly and environmentally destructive legacy of plastic trash.

Because plastics usually either float or are neutrally buoyant, they are easily mistaken for food by aquatic animals and birds. A common cause of sea turtle death is the ingestion of plastic — they mistake plastic bags for jellyfish, a primary food source. Researchers estimate that more than 15 percent of all seabird species have either eaten plastic or fed it to their young. Styrofoam pellets are a particular problem because of their resemblance to plankton and fish eggs.

When ingested, plastic accumulates in the animal's gut, reducing the sense of hunger and inhibiting feeding. This results in a lowering of fat reserves that may prevent growth, reproduction or migration. Plastic may also cause intestinal and stomach ulceration or contribute synthetic chemicals to body tissues, causing eggshell thinning, aberrant behavior or tissue damage.

Plastic strapping bands and other packaging materials are often found around the necks of marine mammals, cutting the flesh, causing infections and inhibiting breathing or feeding.

Plastic fishing gear, particularly nets, are strong and thin compared to traditional nets. This makes them virtually invisible and indestructible. If lost or discarded, these nets continue to capture and kill fish, seabirds and marine mammals.

Munitions

For many decades, military forces disposed of defective, obsolete or surplus munitions (including some chemical weapons) by dumping them at sea. Although this practice is now regulated, and deliberate dumping in coastal waters is authorized only in emergency situations, enforcement may be inadequate.

The sea floor is littered with the remnants of sunken military ships, many of which contain unexploded ordinance.

Photo by Anthony Ellis

The shallower wrecks (like those in Micronesia's Chuuk Lagoon) pose a hazard to divers who may unknowingly come across live ammunition.

Heat

It seems odd to consider heat a pollution source. In temperate areas, hot water discharge is beneficial, and is used by aquaculture operations to enhance production. But under the wrong circumstances, the effects of heat are as devastating as chemical hazards. A primary source of heat pollution is the cooling water released from coastal power stations and factories. In tropical seas or other warmer-water areas where summer temperatures are already near the maximum thermal tolerance for many organisms, this additional heat can be deadly. Many tropical marine organisms aren't able to withstand a water temperature increase of more than two or three degrees beyond the normal average.

Introduction of Alien Species

Increased maritime trade is an important aspect of the global economy, yet it has brought about unforeseen negative environmental consequences. One problem arising from shipping is the effluent and ballast water that ships eject from their bilges. This

Zebra Mussels (Dreissena polymorpha and D. bugensis) in the Great Lakes, USA

water often contains organisms—both adults and larvae— that may be alien to local ecosystems. Sometimes these organisms die quickly due to temperature or salinity factors, or local predators. Other times, however, the new visitors adapt easily and flourish. Because they have no natural predators, they may eventually out-compete local organisms.

Introducing new species can wreak environmental havoc. Rivers, streams and lakes are especially vulnerable to invasion by alien species. For example, zebra mussels (*Dreissena polymorpha and D. bugensis*), recent unwelcome visitors to North America, appeared in the Great Lakes of Canada and the US in 1988. Their larvae probably arrived in European vessels' ballast water. Scientists believe they originated in the Black Sea or lower Dneiper near the Ukrainian seaports of Kherson and Nikolayev. By 1989, the mussels formed dense clusters – up to 30,000 per square metre/25,083 per square yard – inundating underwater structures and clogging intake pipes. In addition to physical damage, the zebra mussel also poses an ecological threat because they consume the algae that serves as the basis of the local aquatic food chain.

Although bilge water discharge is the primary source of alien species, they can arrive in other ways.

For example, in the 1960s the aquarium trade brought the aquatic weed hydrilla (*Hydrilla verticillata*) to the southeastern United States. Once this weed found its way into the fresh, warm waters of Florida, it became a troublesome invader that smothered and replaced virtually every native bottom plant species in the area.

Some ecologists contend that we are rapidly changing the earth into a one-world homogeneous ecosystem, resulting in the loss of species diversity. They warn that rapid transportation, habitat destruction and alien species introduction spell disaster for many species. While environment changes have occurred throughout history, modern maritime commerce has accelerated the rate to a pace that is hard to adjust to without significant alterations to the biosphere.

FISHERIES CONCERNS

For millennia, humanity assumed the seas held infinite resources. When we needed more to feed growing populations, we took more. However, decreasing species counts and declining catches are obvious signs that the ocean is not "bottomless." Production is finite and technology has made it possible to exhaust living ocean resources.

American biologist Garrett Hardin explained the phenomenon of exploitation in his 1968 article *Tragedy of the Commons*. Hardin described a rural community where all citizens grazed their livestock on a commonly owned field. Like any field, this common area could support a limited number of animals before becoming barren. If each farmer concluded that the immediate personal benefit of adding another animal far outweighed the remote risk of degrading the commons, the field would soon be destroyed. Hardin's point is that abuse of the commons, by one or many, is a tragedy shared proportionally by all.

The oceans that lie outside national borders are sometimes referred to as the *global commons*. The resources available in these global commons can be exploited by any nation because no one (and everyone) owns it. Fishing is almost entirely unregulated and because there is no sense of legal ownership for the ocean commons, nations feel little moral responsibility to manage its resources. The tragedy of the global commons is its vulnerability to environmental abuse.

Worldwide Fisheries

In many developed countries, fish is not a primary food source, but rather an occasional meal. However, for much of the world's population, fish and other seafood are vitally important to daily life. Fish account for almost 16 percent of all animal protein consumed by humans — more than beef,

Photo by Claire Ellis

poultry, pork or any other animal source combined. An estimated one billion people depend on fish as their primary protein source and 39 countries are dependent on fish as a major protein source.

The world's fisheries employ about 200 million people. Worldwide, fisheries produce about 91 million metric tons/100 million tons of fish per year of which more than 80 percent comes from the ocean, about 15 percent from aquaculture and the rest from freshwater sources.

In the last 150 years, ocean fish catches have increased 70-fold and the demand has strained the world's fisheries. Many experts believe that the current annual fish catch can't be sustained. According to the United Nation's Food and Agricultural Organization (FAO), the world fishing fleet doubled from 585,000 to 1.2 million large boats between 1970 and 1990. Yet annual fish catches have remained

THE LAW OF THE SEA

The origins of sea law can be traced back to 1493 when Pope Alexander VI issued the Bull of Demarcation. The Bull of Demarcation divided the New World between Spain and Portugal, thus giving these two major powers exclusive trading privileges with the East and West Indies.

Not much happened to advance the concept of the law of the sea during the intervening 116 years. However in 1609, chapter 12 of noted Dutch theorist Hugo Grotius' book *De Jure Praedae* (Commentary on the Law of Prize and Booty) was published as *Mare Liberum* (The Freedom of the Seas). The work defended free access to the sea for all nations.

More than a hundred years later, this idea was formally recognized with the creation of a five kilometre/three mile boundary called the "territorial sea" over which coastal nations had complete sovereignty. Outside the territorial sea was a region belonging to no nation — the high seas. Since then, the legal reasoning put forth in *Mare Liberum* and its conventions, have formed the basis of all modern international sea laws.

In 1945, the Truman Proclamation challenged the traditional definition of the territorial sea. After World War II, new technologies made oil and natural gas accessible on the United States' continental shelf, beyond the five kilometre/three mile limit. To protect these resources, President Harry Truman issued a unilateral proclamation annexing the physical and biological resources of the continental shelf adjacent to the United States. Other nations quickly followed suit. Although the Proclamation had no basis in international law, there was little objection to it, and it became the source of further international continental shelf regulation.

In 1953, the Outer Continental Shelf Lands Act was signed into law, granting control of the seabed and subsoil of the outer continental shelf to the US federal government. This legislation was partially motivated by a 1952 document called the Declaration on the Maritime Zone that extended Chile, Ecuador and Peru's jurisdiction and sovereignty over the sea, seabed and subsoil for 350 kilometres/200 miles from their respective coastlines.

Sparked by international disputes over these drastic changes in time-honored maritime law, the United Nations (UN) convened the Law of the Sea Conference in Geneva, Switzerland in 1958. It took 24 years, but in April 1982 the UN adopted the Convention of the Law of the Sea (UNCLOS). By 1988, more than 140 countries had signed all or most parts of the treaty and it went into effect in 1994.

The Convention established exclusive economic zones (EEZs) extending 370 kilometres/200 nautical miles from a nation's shoreline. Within its EEZ, a nation holds sovereignty over resources, economic activity and environmental protection. Ocean areas outside the EEZs are considered international waters, or common property shared by the world's citizens. The net effect of the Convention was to place about 40 percent of the world's oceans within the EEZs and under the control of coastal nations.

static or declined since 1989.

What is perhaps most unbelievable is that it costs the worldwide fishing industry $124 billion US per year to operate boats, pay staff, buy fuel and maintain equipment, yet it catches only $70 billion worth of fish. That's a $54 billion deficit.

How does this happen? Governments subsidize the fishing industry through fuel-tax exemptions, low-interest loans, price controls and grants using the rationale that spending more to earn less is justified because it preserves employment. This assistance props up the world's massive fishing fleet allowing it to catch fish at an alarming rate.

The Collapse

Along with economic difficulties, the world's fisheries face problems caused by environmental and biological decline. Pollution and habitat destruction interfere with reproduction, but the major concern is that more fish are taken from the ocean than are produced.

Since the 1980s, 70 percent of the world's food fish species have become either overfished, fished to capacity or are rebuilding from overfishing. The United Nation's FAO estimates that of the 17 major fishery areas in the world, four are depleted and the other 13 are again either fished to capacity or overfished.

It's easy to assume overfishing is a developing nation problem due to economic and population pressures. However, the overfishing crisis stems from actions by both developing and developed countries. Five of the eight regions where fish stocks are under heaviest pressure — the northwest and northeast Atlantic, the Mediterranean and the northwest and northeast Pacific — are under the jurisdiction of developed nations. Two of the remaining three—the eastern central and southeast Atlantic—are dominated by fishing fleets from developed countries.

Photo by NOAA/Department of Commerce

Photo by NOAA/Department of Commerce

France, Japan, Norway, Spain and Russia dominate the eastern central Atlantic, with South Korea operating the only major fleet there from a developing nation. Japan, Poland, Spain, Russia and South Africa operates the largest fleets in the southeast Atlantic, with Cuba operating the sole major developing country fleet. The single exception is the southeast Pacific where Peru and Chile do most of the fishing.

Bycatch

Overfishing doesn't just involve the fish that reach your grocer's display cases. Commercial marine fisheries discard nearly 24 million metric tons/27 million tons of nontarget fish, seabirds, sea turtles, marine mammals and other ocean life each year as *bycatch* – the catch that is incidental to the target. Since most bycatch is killed,

> **RIPPLE EFFECT**
> A fishery collapse in one area affects the entire world. A case in point is Peru's once-thriving anchovy fishery. At one time the world's largest fishery, its collapse in 1972 due to weather fluctuations caused by El Niño Southern Oscillation (ENSO) cost Peru two of its major export commodities – fish meal and guano from the sea birds dependent on anchovy. The anchovy collapse resulted in a stifling external debt for Peru and the worldwide loss of a major protein supplement used to feed swine and poultry. This caused a substantial rise in global meat prices.

some conservationists call it *bykill*.

Bycatch accounts for one-third of the total world fish catch. For some fisheries bycatch is higher. For example, some shrimp trawlers discard 80-90 percent of their catch. This equates to eight kilograms/pounds of bycatch discarded for every kilogram/pound of shrimp that makes it to the market.

In the 1980s, dolphins being destroyed as bycatch in tuna nets drew worldwide attention. Since then public pressure, legislation and international agreements have led to revised fishing practices that dramatically reduced the number of dolphins killed each year. Although some dolphins are still caught in tuna nets, this effort proves it is possible to lessen bycatch through improved fishing techniques and technology.

Fishing Practices

Technological advances have made us too good at catching fish. In the past, as competition increased and fish populations decreased, the fishing industry found advanced, and often more damaging, methods to sustain catch levels. Technology allows factory freezer trawlers to process fish on site and stay out on the open seas for a month or more. Today, finding fish is not a matter of luck, but rather a skilled process using radar, sonar, satellite technology and aircraft. A few of the more destructive fishing practices include:

- *Long-lines* — lines stretching out 130 kilometres/80 miles or more with thousands of baited hooks – allow fishing boats to reel in huge catches. Unfortunately, nontarget fish and sea birds are often hooked as bycatch.

- *Gill/Drift nets* – mesh nets up to 65 kilometres/40 miles long – are the most common commercial fishing gear. These large nets efficiently trap the target fish,  but also drown nontarget species and marine mammals at the same time.

- *Pair Trawling/Seining* – two boats operating in tandem towing a net – is a relatively new and highly efficient fishing technique. By lowering nets to the best depth for target fish, the boats corral and haul up record catches.

- *Bottom Trawling/Dredging* – dragging the sea floor to collect bottom dwellers causes physical damage by destroy-

Healthy Sea Floor (top) and Sea Floor Damaged by Trawling (bottom)

ing structures and stirring up silt. Everything is scooped up and nontarget species are dumped over the side. Heavily dredged areas show little biodiversity because only hardy species can survive the regular disturbances.

- *Explosives* – bombs, often homemade, detonated near reefs – stun or kill not only the desired fish, but everything surrounding the charge. The death of invertebrates, juvenile fish and corals weaken the ecosystem, sometimes beyond recovery. Sadly, these practices are so commonplace in some areas that they've become part of the fishing community's "traditional culture."
- *Poisons* – usually cyanide – are used to temporarily paralyze fish so they may be taken live. Driven mainly by aquarium and live fish restaurant trades, poison use is a major issue in biologically rich areas, such as the Indo-Pacific region. Poisons often result in a 50 percent mortality rate to fish and damage the coral reefs that serve as spawning grounds and habitats for many food fish. It's estimated that this industry has grown to become a $1 billion US industry, taking 18-23 metric tons/20-25 tons of live fish annually, and killing many more.

Shark Fisheries — Recipe for Disaster

Most fish species spawn several times a year, dispensing tens to hundreds of thousands of eggs into the water. The strategy is to produce enough larvae so that even with high mortality, enough survive and develop into full-grown fish.

Shark Egg Case

For sharks, however, the reproductive strategy is different and very diverse. Some sharks are *oviparous*, meaning they produce eggs that hatch outside the mother's body. Other sharks, like the sand tiger, develop eggs internally, but with no connection to the uterus. This is called *aplacental viviparity* and the young are born alive after the eggs hatch internally. Many sharks, however, reproduce more like humans. They develop a yolksac placenta from which the embryo receives nutrients. This is called *placental viviparity*.

Shark *gestation*, the period between conception and birth, is also more like mammals than fish. Some species have a gestation of more than a year. In fact, the spiny dogfish (*Squalus acanthias*) has the longest

© Jeremy Stafford-Dietsch

gestation of any known vertebrate — 20-24 months.

Sharks also develop slowly and reach sexual maturity at a very late age compared to other animals. Lemon sharks (*Negaprion brevirostris*), for example, take an average of 15 years to sexually mature. The sandbar shark (*Carcharhinus plumbeus*) — perhaps the most important commercial species in the Atlantic — doesn't reach sexual maturity for nearly 20 years.

Even with differing reproductive systems, gestations and development rates, the one unifying factor among all sharks is that they produce few offspring.

Why? Sharks have few natural predators, thus the survival of young animals is likely thereby reducing the need to put energy into producing a number of babies.

Unfortunately, the problem is that humans have become serious predators through efficient shark fishing practices. The shark's highly effective reproductive strategy cannot keep up with the numbers being caught and killed. Taking sharks before they can reproduce virtually guarantees their destruction.

Adding to their plight, some shark species congregate in nearshore nursery grounds to give birth. Young sharks often remain in these areas for years. The survival of a healthy population depends on protecting these threatened habitats. An added pressure on some species such as blue sharks (*Prionace glauca*) is their tendency to swim in groups of the same sex. This behavior enables fishers to remove large numbers of mature females, leaving little hope for future generations.

Historically, large-scale shark fisheries have not done well, yet the shark fishing trade remains. Although it's difficult to determine the total worldwide catch, an estimated 30 to more than 100 million sharks are killed each year. In 1991 alone, reported landings rose to a record 638,658 metric tons/704,000 tons. Sadly, many sharks are taken only to be *finned*— the practice of cutting off the dorsal, caudal and pectoral fins and then discarding the shark, sometimes still alive, into the sea to drown.

However, catch estimates do not include the primary cause of shark mortality — bycatch. When bycatch and unreported landing estimates are added, the actual total is more than 1,270,058 metric tons/1,400,000 tons a year.

Shark fishing is largely unregulated. No interna-

PROTECT THE SHARKS

People often think of sharks as vicious killing machines. Movies, such as *Jaws*, as well as fictional stories and dramatic television programs help foster this misconception. In reality, of the approximately 400 species of sharks, only 21 are considered a threat to humans. Those who go in and under water – swimmers, snorkelers and scuba divers – are at minimal risk.

Lightning, alligators, bee stings and farm animals kill more people independently than sharks every year. Worldwide, less than 100 shark attacks are reported annually, and of these, only 15 percent are fatal. The truth is, sharks are in far greater danger from humans than we are from them. For every person attacked by a shark, approximately one million sharks are killed.

The fact is sharks are in need of help. Sharks perform vitally important biological functions in the ecosystem and without them we would disturb nature's critical balance. Having survived for more than 400 million years, it is devastating to learn that humans may soon cause some species to become extinct.

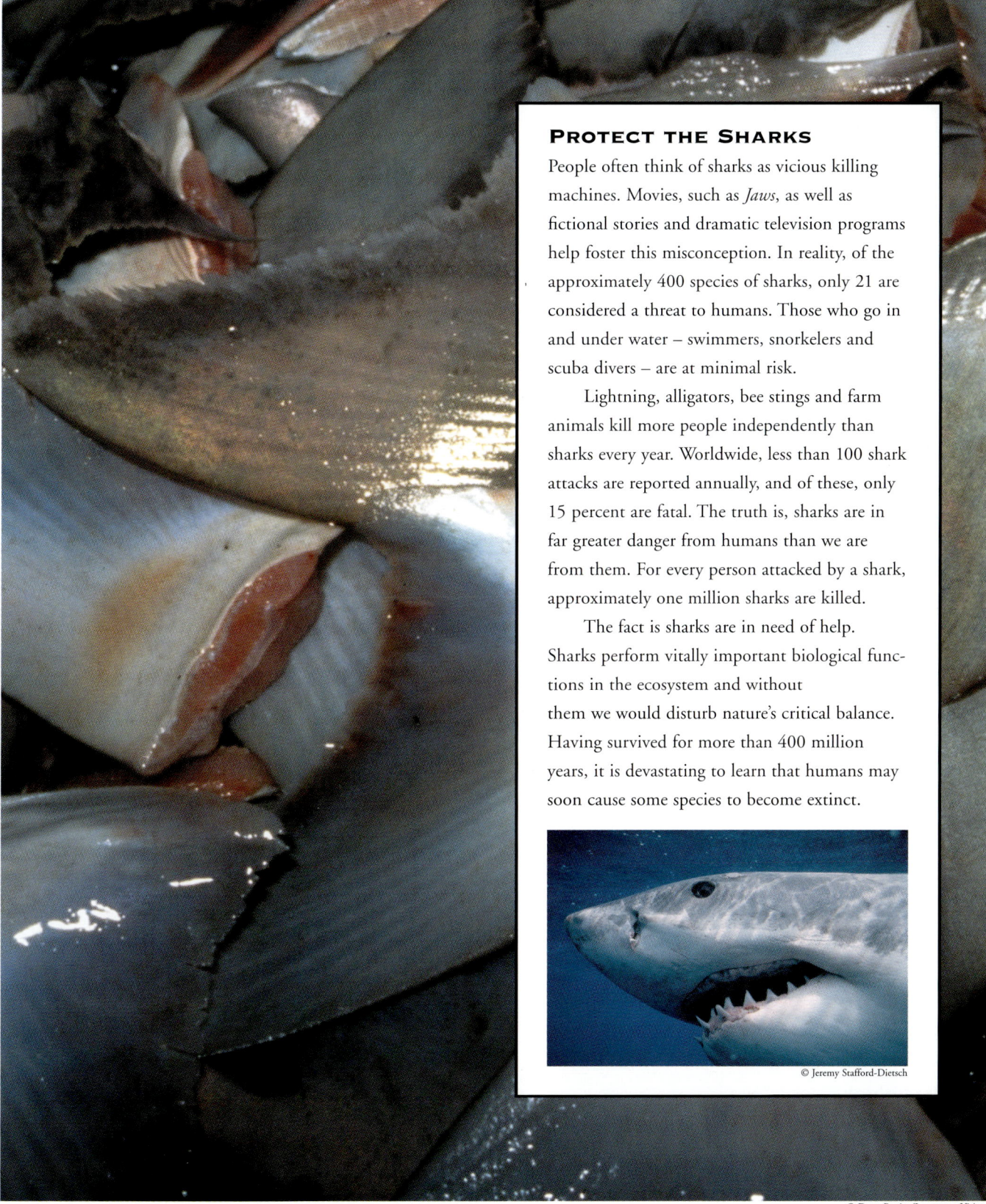

© Jeremy Stafford-Dietsch

© Doug Perrine/Innerspace Visions

tional management plans currently exist for sharks. To date, only four countries in the world — the United States, South Africa, Australia and the United Kingdom — have domestic shark management plans. However, a few other countries are beginning to take protective steps. For example, in 1998, the Maldivian government banned shark fishing in all seven of its tourist atolls for 10 years, thereby affirming sharks' importance to that country's economy as a living resource rather than a harvested one.

Even in countries where shark management plans exist, there's concern that targeted shark species are not recovering as planned. Management decisions sometimes fail to account for shark's low reproductive rates. Scientists regularly advise significant reductions in catches and some believe that any catch at all inhibits the recovery of large coastal shark populations.

An important issue is that no resource management plan can work without public support. Through educational programs, such as Project AWARE's Protect the Sharks campaign, people can learn about sharks' contribution to the health of the oceans and help protect them. We must balance short-term economic interests with long-term conservation strategies.

Future Outlook

In response to declining fish stocks, an increasing number of non-traditional species like capelin, sprat and Pacific pollock are being introduced. This shift increases productivity but creates problems in the marketplace because people are reluctant to buy unfamiliar fish. More importantly, these new fisheries may have negative effects on traditional stocks because of yet-unknown interactions.

Many believe another approach to the overfishing problem is to stop catching fish and start growing them. *Aquaculture*, or fish farming, does offer some hope of reducing the pressure on worldwide fisheries. Since the 1960s, fish and shellfish production from aquaculture has increased three-fold.

However, aquaculture is not problem-free. Large numbers of fish grown within small ponds produce high levels of concentrated waste. In addition, fish living in such

© NOAA/Department of Commerce

close proximity are prone to disease and nutritional problems, so farmers often add steroids, vitamins and antibiotics to the ponds. In systems where the ponds lead to open water, these substances are introduced into the environment, and the long-term consequences are often unknown. Another concern is that vast areas of coastal wetlands, especially mangrove forests, are destroyed to build aquaculture facilities. This is a particular problem in the shrimp farming industries of South America and Southeast Asia.

COASTAL ZONE AND WETLAND DEGRADATION

Coastal Area Before Development (top) and After a Harbor is Built (bottom)

About two-thirds of the world's six billion people live along ocean coastlines. In developed countries, it's driven by desire, and in developing nations, it's often necessary for employment and food. In the US alone, 70 percent of the population lives within a day's drive of the coast and many of the world's largest metropolitan areas are found directly within the coastal zone.

It's no surprise that coastal waters receive the major portion of land-derived waste, ranging from sewage to toxic materials. Besides the constant influx of pollutants, coastal areas face physical damage as more structures are built. Jetties, seawalls, piers and bridges interfere with water and sediment circulation. This alters longshore sediment transport, causing coastal erosion and other habitat disturbances.

Because coastal areas are viewed as prime real estate, tidal flats, marshes and beaches are filled in for residential

101

SHRINKING FRESHWATER RESOURCES

Excessive water demands, due to population growth, are responsible for lowering water tables, shrinking of inland seas, lakes and estuaries and degradation resulting from altered flow patterns in rivers and streams. Groundwater depletion, urbanization and destructive land use practices such as deforestation and overgrazing also contribute to the loss of freshwater ecosystems. Sewage outfall and other pollution turn abundant resources into unusable messes.

When groundwater is withdrawn too quickly or stream flow is redirected or reduced, the results can be disastrous — wetlands, bogs and ponds dry up and the overlying land may recede or sink, damaging streets and buildings.

Examples include:

- *The Aral Sea, bordering Kazakhstan and Uzbekistan* — Until recent times, it was the world's fourth largest lake and although it is still a sizable inland body of water, large withdrawals have caused it to shrink by 40 percent. The rivers that feed the Aral Sea now irrigate cotton fields and rice paddies in Uzbekistan, Turkmenistan and Tajikistan. The loss of inflow caused a 18 metre/59 foot water drop since the 1960's.
- *The Caspian Sea* — It experienced a water level drop of more than three metres/ten feet over the past 50 years primarily due to damming and diversions for irrigation on the Volga River. Its water level continues to fall.
- *North and East Africa* — At least 10 countries are experiencing severe water shortages. Egypt is already near its limit and could lose vital supplies from the Nile as upper-basin nations (countries to the south) develop the river's headwaters.
- *China* — One-third of all the water in China's major rivers is polluted beyond safe levels. Fifty cities face acute water shortages. Water tables beneath Beijing are dropping by up to two metres/ six feet per year. Farmers in the Beijing region could lose 30 to 40 percent of their current water supply to domestic and industrial use.
- *India* — Tens of thousands of villages now face freshwater shortages and plans to divert water from the Brahmaputra River have increased Bangladesh's fear of shortages. Large portions of New Delhi have water for only a few hours each day.
- *Latin America* — Almost all municipal sewage and industrial effluents are discharged into the nearest river or stream. Mexico City suffers from subsidence because groundwater pumping exceeds recharge by 40 percent in some areas.
- *The Middle East* — Water shortages are imminent in all areas except for Israel, Jordan and the West Bank – countries that are making great strides in using all renewable sources. Syria lost vital freshwater supplies when Turkey's massive Ataturk Dam went operational.
- *The United States* — One-fifth of the total irrigated land is watered by excessive pumping of groundwater. Too much water is being drained from roughly half of all western rivers. To augment supplies cities are buying farmers' water rights which only exacerbates the problem.

housing, commercial enterprises and even airports. Estuaries are doubly endangered because they are often dredged for use as harbors. Poor land use practices, such as deforesting coastal regions for logging or agriculture, poorly managed dredge and fill projects, dam building and destruction of sand dunes for coastal development all contribute to the rapid disappearance of coastal wetlands.

In the tropics, mangrove destruction is a serious concern. Mangrove is a general term used to describe a variety of tropical inshore ecosystems dominated by several species of trees or shrubs that grow in salt water. At one time, 60-75 percent of the earth's tropical coastline and semi-tropical regions were lined with mangrove forests, but not any longer. It's estimated that mangroves now occupy less than 50 percent of their original range and are disappearing faster than tropical rainforests.

In many parts of Southeast Asia and South America, for example, large areas of mangroves were chopped down to build aquaculture ponds, or for use as firewood or charcoal.

© NOAA/Department of Commerce

QUIZ

1. What are the major sources of pollution entering the aquatic environment? (choose all that apply)
   a. propellants, hydrocarbons and biocides.
   b. agricultural and industrial runoff.
   c. industrial, municipal or agricultural waste dumping and dredge spoils.
   d. maritime accidents or ships dumping bilge water, ballast water and garbage.
2. True or False. Most oil enters the aquatic environment from land-based sources, such as runoff from parking lots and structures and effluent from wastewater treatment plants.
3. Plastics in the aquatic environment: (choose all that apply)
   a. are sometimes mistaken by animals as food.
   b. may not degrade for hundreds of years.
   c. entrap or strangle fish, mammals and birds.
   d. always float and wash up on shore.
4. True or False. Because there is generally no sense of legal ownership for the ocean commons, nations often feel little moral responsibility to manage its limited resources.
5. True or False. Many fisheries face collapse due to pollution, habitat destruction and overfishing.
6. Bycatch may include: (choose all that apply)
   a. sea birds and marine mammals.
   b. turtles.
   c. target fish species.
   d. nontarget fish.
7. What are some of today's most destructive fishing practices? (choose all that apply)
   a. Long-lines
   b. Poisons
   c. Explosives
   d. Fly fishing
8. Approximately _____ of the world's population live along ocean coastline.
   a. 1/3
   b. 1/2
   c. 2/3
   d. 3/4
9. True or False. Coastal wetlands are often destroyed because they have great economic potential as prime real estate.

How did you do? 1. a, b, c and d; 2. True 3. a, b and c; 4. True; 5. True; 6. a, b and d; 7. a, b and c; 8. c; 9. True.

CHAPTER SIX
TROUBLED WATERS—
OTHER DEGRADED AQUATIC ENVIRONMENTS

THE WORLD'S MOST ENVIRONMENTALLY THREATENED REGIONS

TROUBLED WATERS— OTHER DEGRADED AQUATIC ENVIRONMENTS

The World's Most Environmentally Threatened Regions
- The Mediterranean Sea
- The Strait of Malacca
- The North Sea
- The Baltic Sea
- The Persian Gulf
- The Caribbean Sea

STUDY QUESTIONS
Underline/highlight the answers to these questions as you read:
1. Where are the world's most environmentally threatened regions?
2. What are the main factors or conditions that threaten these regions?

To a degree, every fresh and salt water resource on the planet faces environmental threats. However, the problems, their effects and the severity of environmental decline vary by region. It's not surprising that regions under the most serious threat are those bordered by growing populations or used extensively for shipping.

Many threatened regions continue to supply local human residents and visitors with aquatic resources – both economic and recreational – yet the ability of these troubled waters to ward off ever-increasing environmental pressures is concerning. A few of these areas offer good diving and snorkeling and are central to the region's tourism; however, their popularity is often a contributing factor to their decline.

According to the United Nations Environmental Programme (UNEP), the world's most environmentally threatened marine regions are:
- The Mediterranean Sea
- The Straits of Malacca
- The North Sea
- The Baltic Sea
- The Persian Gulf
- The Caribbean Sea

Fortunately, aquatic ecosystems show an astonishing ability to recover if given a chance. However, before any area can recover, we must correct or minimize the environmental threat, then give the system time to heal. The current state of the following regions is serious, but not hopeless.

The Mediterranean

Human civilization has lived along the sea the Romans referred to as *Mare Nostrum* (our sea) for thousands of years. Throughout history, surrounding people dumped their waste into the Mediterranean and the sea "processed" it.

However, today the Mediterranean's ability to handle waste is being tested. Untreated or inadequately treated sewage flows into its waters from more than 120 coastal cities and each year thousands of tons of industrial waste and agricultural chemicals reach the sea. Chronically high levels of pollution have been

© Michel Verdure

recorded throughout the entire Mediterranean Sea, including the northern Adriatic Sea, Greece's Elevsis Bay, Turkey's Izmir Bay, Tunisia's Tunis Lagoon and the near-shore waters of Alexandria, Egypt.

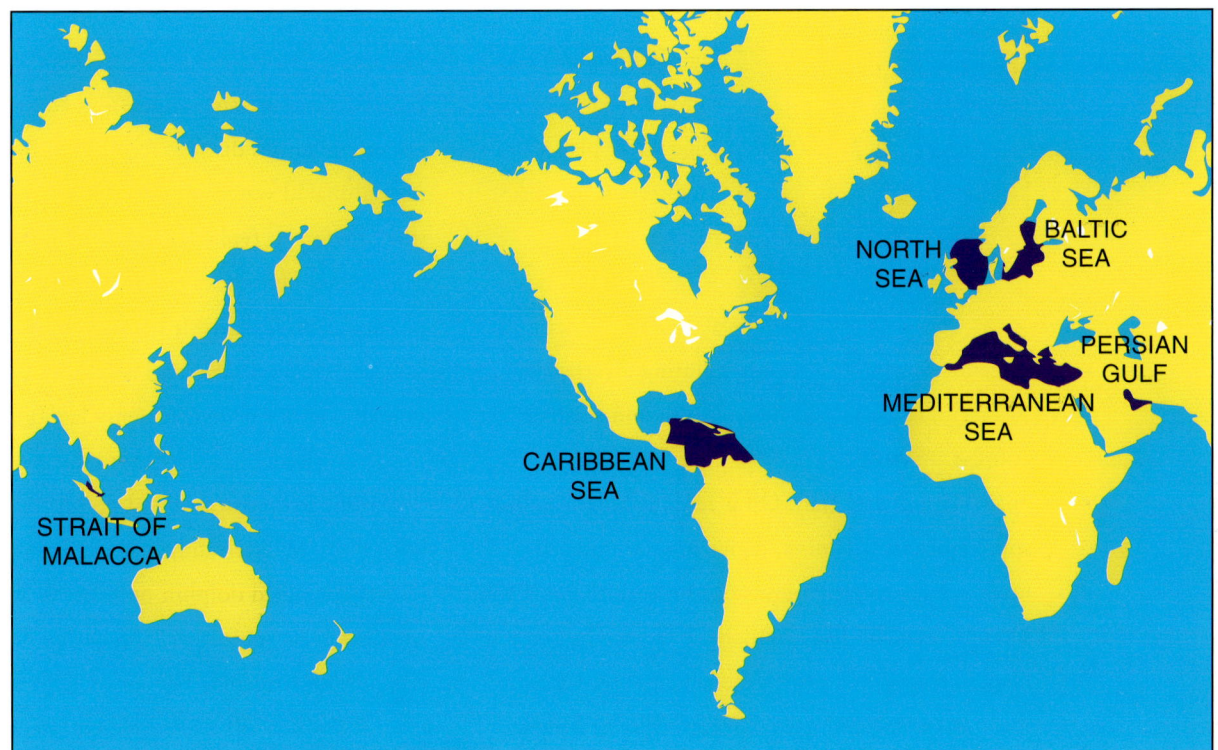

Six of the World's Most Environmentally Threatened Regions

Petroleum

Oil pollution is a major problem in the Mediterranean. Though this sea accounts for only one percent of the world's ocean surface, 22 percent of the planet's oil, some 544 million metric tons/600 million tons of petroleum products, travel across the Mediterranean each year. It's estimated that more than 453,592 metric tons/600,000 tons of oil enter the sea from spillage and ballasting operations. This does not include the 226,796 metic tons/250,000 tons of petroleum-based pollutants that enter the Mediterranean from land-based sources.

© Ecoscene

Shipping also contributes to the Mediterranean's pollution in ways that have far-reaching effects on the region's major economic activity – tourism. Tar from de-ballasting, tank-washing of oil tankers and ships' discharge of oily bilge water plague Mediterranean beaches.

Oil pollution also affects fisheries, tainting a variety of finfish and shellfish near port cities in Spain, France and Italy. Oil is responsible for killing spiny lobsters in Tunisia, damaging bonito and mackerel spawning grounds on the Turkish coast and severely reducing fish populations in the Gulf of Naples, Cagliari and the Venetian lagoons. One of the worst examples may be Trieste's Bay of Muggia. This once-thriving bay is now virtually a biological desert because of petrochemical pollution.

The Mediterranean is unique in that it is almost completely landlocked — open to the ocean only through the Straits of Gibraltar and the Suez Canal. This has important environmental consequences because it means the Mediterranean cannot quickly disperse waste. In fact, it takes 80-100 years to completely recycle all the water in the Mediterranean Sea.

Pollutants

Pollution is a pressing concern in coastal areas, because it causes diseases transferred by either contaminated water or seafood, such as viral hepatitis, dysentery, typhoid and cholera. Today, many beaches are periodically closed because they are public health hazards. It is unsafe to eat seafood caught in certain areas and algae blooms or low oxygen conditions render many lagoons and estuaries "dead."

Habitat destruction and pollution has taken a toll on the Mediterranean's marine mammals with a severely depleted dolphin population and the Mediterranean monk seal (*Monachus monachus*) now critically endangered. The monk seals now range from the waters off a few isolated Greek islands, to the Aegean coast of Turkey with remnant populations off Morocco and Algeria.

Waste flowing from industrial centers is also a significant concern. The waters near the Mediterranean's population centers now contain high levels of industrial waste and heavy metals.

Warfare
Disruption caused by intermittent warfare in the eastern Mediterranean strains relations and stalls cooperative efforts. Political and social concerns easily overshadow the critical decision-making necessary to sustain the region's environmental health.

Strait of Malacca

The Strait of Malacca is a small region off Indonesia between Sumatra and West Malaysia. It offers the fastest route from the Indian Ocean to the South China Sea, which is what places it in environmental jeopardy. Nearly all Persian Gulf oil headed for Japan passes through the Strait and because Japan imports 85 percent of its oil from the Middle East, the tanker traffic volume is enormous.

More than 4300 fully-loaded tankers carrying an estimated 272 million metric tons/300 million tons of oil and petrochemical products pass through the Strait yearly. The congestion inevitably results in accidents and oil spills. In an eight year period there were 43 incidents involving oil tankers – ten of which released oil.

Besides accidental spills, tankers also flush oil-contaminated water from their ballast tanks before entering the Strait's eastern passage. Because the

© Ecoscene

Strait is shallow, tankers prefer to ride high and pump out extra weight to reduce their drafts. Some environmentalists suspect that prevailing winds and currents carry this oil into the Strait's most productive fishing areas.

Further complicating matters, Singapore, which is located on the Strait's eastern end, is one of the world's largest refinery centers. Along with refinery operations come the inevitable spills and accidents at coastal docking operations.

Beaches in the Strait of Malacca are commonly speckled with tar, and not surprisingly, fisheries productivity has declined.

The North Sea

The North Sea has always been one of the world's busiest marine regions. The Straits of Dover and the southern North Sea host heavily trafficked shipping lanes. Gravel and sand dredging operations occupy the region and oil and gas platforms abound. The highly productive fishing grounds are intensely exploited.

Waste

More than 30 million people call the North Sea's industrialized coastline home. Human-produced waste empties into the North Sea from several major rivers, which collectively drain an area of nearly 850,000 square kilometres/331,500 square miles. Most sewage flows into the North Sea untreated, or with only primary treatment, which removes only solid materials.

This region also contains the largest assemblage of industrial plants on earth, accounting for 15 percent of the world's industrial output. Since the industrial revolution, huge quantities of industrial wastes have flowed into the North Sea

Petroleum

Busy shipping lanes mean accidents and oil spills. One of the worst occurred on 16 March 1978, the oil tanker *Amoco*

Cadiz ran aground off the coast of France spilling 264 million litres/70 million gallons of oil into the water. The slick produced by the sixth largest oil spill in history was eight times the size of the one formed when the *Exxon Valdez* ran aground in Alaska, USA in 1989.

Even more oil enters the North Sea from platforms and shipping operations, small-scale accidents or ballast and bilge water discharge from ships. Small oil slicks are not uncommon in the region.

Aquatic Life
Overfishing, habitat destruction and pollutants all endanger the regions' aquatic life and have caused species numbers to dwindle. Overfishing has led to the collapse of some long-standing fisheries. Sand and gravel dredging continue to destroy the North Sea's once vital spawning habitats leading to lower production.

The turbidity from dredging in combination with siltation from local rivers, smothers bottom dwellers and releases toxic materials into the environment. As a result, monitoring heavy metal concentration in seafood taken from the North Sea is required.

In addition to its underwater life, the North Sea is home to large resident bird populations and serves as a wintering ground for many shore and sea birds. Oil pollution spells disaster for birds and each winter kills many of them. Development of coastal wetlands and shallows, destruction of feeding grounds and depletion of fish stocks by commercial overfishing, all spell trouble for the region's once-thriving bird populations.

The Baltic Sea
The Baltic Sea's problems stem from the fact that its drainage area is four times the size of the sea itself, and its shores hold thousands of highly polluting industries and population

© Bret Forbes

© Ecoscene

centers. Because the sea's average depth is only 60 metres/200 feet and it takes 30 years for its waters to cycle, the Baltic has difficulty processing incoming pollutants.

The Baltic Sea is unique in that its brackish surface water floats on a denser, saltier, deeper water mass. Although the layers mix somewhat during the fall and winter, there is a permanent *halocline* (salt water layer) at between 40-60 metres/130-200 feet. Below the halocline, water stagnates as bacterial decay of organic material uses up the available oxygen. Extensive areas with *anoxic* (no oxygen) conditions create dead zones where fish disappear and everything that can die, does.

Eutrophication
The Baltic Sea also has the distinction of being the worst eutrophic site in modern times. *Eutrophication* is a set of physical, chemical and biological changes brought about when excessive nutrients are released into a body of water. Although some eutrophication may benefit fisheries by providing additional food sources, too much leads to a decrease in the prevalence of more highly-prized predatory fish.

In May and June 1988, in the waters between Denmark, Sweden, and Norway, high nutrient pollution levels and warm weather resulted in a monstrous toxic algae bloom. The bloom quickly spread to cover more than 75,000 square kilometres/28,900 square miles. As the blooms died, bacterial decay consumed huge quantities of oxygen covering nearly 1000 kilometres/650 miles of coastline with the rotting remains of millions of marine organisms.

The sea's eutrophication problem results from the large quantity of organic wastes spilling into its waters from the 25 million people on its shores, and the 50 million more people who live within 200 kilometres/124 miles of its coastline. Forty percent of this waste reaches the Baltic untreated.

Chemical and heavy metal pollution
High concentrations of mercury and high levels of cadmium, lead, zinc and copper are found in the Baltic's water and bottom sediments. Since the 1960s, mercury concentrations in finfish cause periodic fisheries closure in the coastal areas of Denmark, Finland and Sweden. The mercury arrives with waste from the pulp, paper and timber industry. It's used in chemicals that kill fungus and slime.

Today, closer monitoring of the marine ecosystem is leading to less mercury contamination. In addition, fish samples have also shown less contamination from other heavy metals.

Halogenated hydrocarbons, however, continue to be a problem. There is considerable concern for the Baltic Sea's wildlife due to levels of dichlorodiphenyltrichloroethane (DDT) and polychlorinated biphenyls (PCBs). Currently, contamination of fish by these chemicals is not high, but bioaccumulation raises the DDT and PCBs level in fish-eating birds and mammals. For example, one study in the 1970s showed concentrations in seals and birds were 10 times higher in the Baltic than in areas west of Sweden. Fortunately, the situation has improved, but there's still much to be done before the region earns a clean bill of health.

The Persian Gulf

Many factors contribute to the Persian Gulf's reputation as one of the world's most abused marine regions. The first is that according to UNEP, its coastline is one of the most rapidly developing regions on earth due to its central role in global oil production and shipment. Life-giving estuaries, coral reefs and tidal communities are replaced by the infra-

Photo by Jack Archibald

structure required to support oil production and an ever-growing population. Thanks to oil revenues, industrialization in the eight Persian Gulf nations is on the rise. This leads to massive dredging to create new harbors and for coastal in-filling.

Along with growth comes the increasing need for fresh water. The region already has the world's largest concentration of desalinization plants, which discharge residual brine into the gulf, raising salinity. Higher salinity, in some habitats, threatens organisms sensitive to these altered conditions.

© Ecoscene

The Persian Gulf's small size and shallow depth are major contributing factors because they prevent the gulf from absorbing the increasing influx of pollutants. The maximum depth is 91 metres/300 feet, the average depth is 34 metres/110 feet and the gulf contains vast areas less than 10 metres/33 feet deep.

The gulf connects to the open ocean through the Strait of Hormuz – a channel that is only 50 kilometres/30 miles wide. The strait is too narrow to effectively flush pollutants to the open ocean and its width forces oil tankers to pass in close proximity. Because more than 60 percent of the world's oil production sails though this bottleneck, there's enormous potential for environmental disasters.

The Persian Gulf's shallow depth does let sunlight penetrate to the bottom, fueling extensive phytoplankton production, which in turn sup-ports a large and varied fishery. However, human-induced changes are causing fish catches to decline. Also, the constant development of new industries and expanding urban centers creates waste so that today, fish show increasing levels of mercury, lead and pollution-related diseases.

The final factor that has hindered attempts to rejuvenate this region is recent warfare. The 1991 Persian Gulf War, the 10 year Iran-Iraq war and other disturbances add pressure to the gulf's already strained ecosystem.

The Caribbean Sea

With its beautiful sandy beaches and warm, clear water, it's surprising for many people to learn that the Caribbean Sea is under significant threat. According to UNEP, from an environmental perspective, this

© Michel Verdure

region is one of the ocean's most polluted and endangered areas. The Nature Conservancy confirms that the Caribbean basin has the highest proportion of deforested land in the Western Hemisphere and the problems assoc-iated with resulting runoff.

Almost 40 percent of all vertebrate species that became extinct in modern times called the Caribbean home. For example, the Caribbean monk seal (*Monachus tropicalis*) became extinct by the mid-1950s. Also, continuing coastal development and accompanying pollution have destroyed much of the remaining habitat of the endangered West Indian manatee (*Trichechus manatus*).

Pesticides, Chemicals and Oil
The Caribbean is the most pesticide-damaged sea on earth, largely as a result of agricultural runoff from croplands in Mexico and the United States. In fact, 41 percent of the land in the US drains down the Mississippi River to the Gulf of Mexico and from there into the Caribbean Sea. The island nations in the region contribute chemical residue from crops such as coffee, cotton, bananas, sugar, cocoa and citrus fruit. Other wastes come from heavy industries that smelt iron, steel and aluminum, or that produce

© Bret Forbes

caustic chemicals like chlorine.

In addition to pesticides and chemicals, oil represents a significant threat to the region. While the Caribbean is often associated with sun, surf and sand, it has the potential to become one of the world's most prolific oil-producing regions. Currently, there are more than 2000 fixed, offshore oil platforms in US Gulf of Mexico waters and more under construction in the oil-producing areas of Trinidad and Tobago, Venezuela and the Gulf of Mexico. Blowouts, overflows, pipeline fractures and other platform accidents are major sources of oil pollution in this area. Additional sources include tanker accidents and oily ballast water discharge.

Tourism

The Caribbean is synonymous with tourism – a trade that brings more than 100 million visitors to the region each year. This is a considerable number, considering that the tiny island nations already have a very high population density.

Supporting a tourism industry requires an infrastructure that brings with it associated environmental consequences. While hotels and other coastal construction release silt and sewage directly into coral reef habitats – only 10 percent of the sewage and industrial waste in the Caribbean is treated.

The ecological balance of many coral reefs is dangerously disturbed due to many tourism activities, including, anchoring, overuse, souvenir collecting and an ever-increasing demand for fish. According to the World Resources Institute, 75 percent of the region's 111,370 square kilometres/43,000 square miles of coral reef are either dead or endangered. Outbreaks of coral disease are now common events.

Quiz

1. According to the United Nations Environmental Programme (UNEP), the world's most environmentally threatened marine regions include: (choose all that apply)
   a. The Mediterranean Sea.
   b. The Strait of Malacca.
   c. The South China Sea.
   d. The Baltic Sea.
   e. The Gulf of Alaska.
   f. The Caribbean Sea.
2. Primary threats that effect many of these regions include:
   a. oil pollution.
   b. population and industry growth.
   c. chemical and heavy metal pollution.
   d. All of the above are correct.

How did you do? 1. a, b, d, and f ; 2. d

CHAPTER SEVEN
CURRENT STATUS AND FUTURE SOLUTIONS

CURRENT STATUS AND FUTURE SOLUTIONS

- **FISHERIES—**
  RESPONSIBLE MANAGEMENT
- **COASTAL ZONE MANAGEMENT**
- **INTERNATIONAL MEASURES**

As daunting as the aquatic environment's problems seem, there's reason to hope for improvement and recovery. The world's fisheries are not yet lost and people are beginning to manage coastal regions more sustainably. Even problems involving water pollution are solvable. It's clear that walking away is not an option and that a large part of the solution involves changing attitude and behavior. Through individual perseverance and cooperative efforts, the environment can survive and recover from its current state.

STUDY QUESTIONS
Underline/highlight the answers to these questions as you read:
1. What steps do environmental organizations believe must be taken to conserve the world's fisheries?
2. What are some examples of effective coastal zone management?
3. What international measures were introduced to eliminate the intentional pollution of the aquatic environment by oil and other harmful discharges from ships?

© Bret Forbes

FISHERIES—
RESPONSIBLE MANAGEMENT

© NOAA/Department of Commerce

With declining marine fish catches and traditional fisheries overfished or fished to capacity, recovery depends on better fisheries management. However, improved fisheries practices alone may not be enough when other factors influence species development and survival.

Loss of coastal wetlands, estuaries and coral reefs or other habitat destruction inhibits reproduction for many fish species and disrupts growth. Perhaps the single most useful step resource managers can take in restoring fish populations and managing fisheries is to revive damaged ecosystems.

Like all environmental problems, restoring the world's fish population requires both local and global action.

Globally, important initiatives are underway. Two of these are the UN Fish Stocks Agreement and the UN Food and Agriculture Organization's Code of Conduct for Responsible Fisheries – both adopted in 1995.

Each initiative has great potential to help reverse the world fisheries crisis, however, only half the countries belonging to the UN have ratified or accepted the agreements at this writing. Obviously, recovery of the world's fish populations can only move forward when more countries seriously commit to solving the problem.

In addition to UN initiatives, nongovernmental organizations, such as the World Wildlife Fund (WWF) and the

WANT TO FISH? KNOW THE RULES

Fishing is a popular recreational activity - one that appears to be growing. When done responsibly, recreational fishing may not affect the environment any more than sustenance fishing which has occurred throughout human history. However, with increasing numbers comes greater potential for abuse.

If you choose to fish, you need to know the local regulations and abide by them. Keep in mind taking an even more conservative approach to recreational fishing than the rules allow may be prudent and beneficial to the aquatic environment.

Before you cast your first line or throw a net, make sure you understand the following local regulations:

- License requirements
- Fish size and weight limits
- Species restrictions
- Daily (period) catch limits
- Area restrictions
- Seasonal restrictions
- Equipment restrictions
- Catch and release procedures (if appropriate)

Marine Fish Conservation Network are working to solve the current fisheries crisis through responsible management plans. Basic principles the WWF include:

1. Establishing and enforcing international minimum fish conservation and management standards.
2. Requiring alternatives to destructive drift net, bottom trawl and long-line fishing gear.
3. Reducing existing economic incentives for unsustainable fishing.
4. Protecting and restoring important marine habitats.
5. Reducing bycatch and nontarget species catches by at least 20 percent by 2005.

Because legislation often moves slowly and widespread enforcement is difficult, local action becomes crucial. Individuals can change the way our fisheries are managed by joining organizations that support science-based fisheries management. On a more personal level, you can also help by making informed seafood purchases as consumers and by being responsible in your own fishing activities.

Photo by Claire Ellis

MAKING RESPONSIBLE SEAFOOD CHOICE

Making informed seafood choices might be the right thing to do, but with so many considerations it is often difficult to decide what to buy. Some species are better able to withstand fishing pressure. By looking through the information on pages 124-127 you will be able to insure that you are making responsible seafood choices.

This information has been provided by the Monterey Bay Aquarium. Because the status of fishers are constantly changing, the Seafood Watch Chart is updated on a quarterly basis. Visit www.mbayaq.org for the current version.

SEAFOOD WATCH CHART

We want to support sustainable fisheries – those that do not overfish, or kill a lot of animals as bycatch, or destroy ocean habitat. Here's the best information we have about fisheries and seafood choices. We will update this chart quarterly as new information becomes available.

This version updated: 17 November 2000.

Primary Data Sources:
U.S. National Marine Fisheries Service
U.N. Food and Agriculture Organization
Australian Bureau of Rural Sciences

Key to "Level of Fishing"
Low level = undeveloped or new fishery
Moderate level = some fishing, fish still plentiful
Fully fished = much fishing, but fish doing OK
Overfished = too much fishing, fish are in danger
Depleted = fish population has crashed
Farmed = raised in aquaculture facilities

Adapted from original version developed by Monterey Bay Aquarium.

Seafood Item	Where's it from?	Level of Fishing	More Information
BEST CHOICES			We look for three things when we choose which fish to buy: a wild population that's abundant enough to sustain fishing; low levels of wasted catch or "bycatch"; and fish caught or farmed in ways that protect the environment.
Albacore/Tombo Tuna	Pacific, Atlantic, Indian Oceans	Fully fished	Almost all of the albacore you will find in the market is from Pacific fisheries, which use hook-and-line methods that result in little or no bycatch. Albacore is overfished in the South Atlantic. In the North Atlantic, Pacific and Indian Oceans, it's considered fully fished.
Calamari strips & steaks (Pacific squid)	New Zealand, China, other Pacific	Low to moderate level	Pacific squid are abundant and the current level of fishing seems to be sustainable.
Calamari, whole (Market squid)	U.S. Pacific Coast	Moderate level	Market squid breed rapidly and their natural life is just one year long. With improved management, market squid could sustain the current level of fishing.
Catfish	United States	Farmed	All catfish you'll find in markets and restaurants is farm-raised. Catfish eat a vegetable-based diet and are raised in freshwater ponds with little impact on the environment.
Clams (New Zealand rock clams or "Steamers")	U.S.; Canada; New Zealand	Farmed	Bivalve aquaculture practices have greatly improved in many areas of the world over the last two decades. We buy farmed clams from a non-polluting source in New Zealand.
Dungeness Crab	N. California	Fully fished	The Dungeness crab fishery is well-managed and healthy. Only large male crabs may be caught, and there's no fishing allowed during the breeding season.
Halibut, Pacific	U.S. Pacific Coast or Alaska	Fully fished	Good management is keeping Pacific halibut populations relatively healthy, but the Atlantic halibut fishery has collapsed. Alaska halibut has the lowest level of bycatch.
Mahi-Mahi (Dorado, Dolphinfish)	Hawaii	Fully fished	Mahi-mahi breed rapidly and can probably withstand a lot of fishing. Populations are healthy, although there is no management plan to prevent future overfishing.
Mussels, Black	U.S.; Canada	Farmed	North American bivalve aquaculture does not appear to have significant environmental impacts and in some cases can improve local water quality. We buy mussels famed around Prince Edward Island.

	Seafood Item	Where's it from?	Level of Fishing	More Information
	Mussels, Green-lipped	New Zealand	Farmed	Bivalve aquaculture practices have improved in many areas of the world over the last two decades. We buy farmed green-lipped mussels from a non-polluting source in New Zealand.
	New Zealand Cod (Hoki)	New Zealand	Fully fished	We use hoki in our fish and chips. It comes from a well-managed fishery that limits the number of fish caught each year.
	Oysters	U.S.; Canada; New Zealand	Farmed	Oyster farming does not appear to have significant environmental impacts and in some cases can improve local water quality. We favor oysters farmed via off-bottom methods (in floating nets or on long oyster lines) as having the least impact on seafloor habitat.
	Rainbow Trout	Idaho	Farmed	Rainbow trout are farmed inland, using closed systems that don't release polluted water.
	Salmon	Alaska, California	Fully fished	We believe wild salmon from a well-regulated fishery is the most environmentally-sound choice. Alaska's wild salmon fisheries are healthy and well-regulated. They were the first fishery in the nation to be certified by the Marine Stewardship Council (September 2000). California's wild-caught salmon are managed effectively. The length of the California salmon season is adjusted to maintain sustainable populations.
	Striped Bass	U.S. West Coast	Farmed	Striped bass are farmed inland, using closed systems that don't release polluted water.

	Seafood Item	Where's it from?	Level of Fishing	More Information
	PROCEED WITH CAUTION			These seafood may or may not be environmentally-friendly, depending on how and where they're caught or farmed. We monitor the status of the wild fish stocks on this list to be sure that populations remain healthy. We check the sources carefully before we buy; we suggest you do the same.
	American Lobster	East Coast N. America	Fully fished to **overfished**	Based on population models and other data, fisheries management agencies list American lobsters as overfished. But the lobster population doesn't seem to be declining; American lobsters are caught in traps with little bycatch; and the fishery is very well regulated. Considering all these factors together, we have moved American lobster from our Avoid list into Proceed with Caution.
	Bay Scallops	New England	Fully fished to **overfished**	Many populations of bay scallops are overfished. We buy bay scallops from Massachusetts, where populations are still healthy.
	Bay Shrimp (Pacific Pink Shrimp)	Pacific Northwest	Moderate to fully fished	The bay shrimp population is healthy. We are trying to learn more about bycatch associated with this fishery.
	English/ Petrale Sole	U.S. West Coast	Moderate to fully fished	Sole populations are healthy, but we're gathering more information about levels of bycatch and habitat impact in this bottom-trawl fishery.
	Imitation Crab/ Surimi (Pollock)	Alaska	Fully fished	Although this is a well-regulated fishery, some scientists believe that heavy pollock fishing takes too much food from sea lions, disrupting Arctic ecosystems. We're studying this issue.

SEAFOOD WATCH CHART

	Salmon	Washington, Oregon	Fully fished	Wild salmon from Washington and Oregon include some healthy and some overfished populations.
	Shrimp/Prawns	Georgia (Turtle Safe)	Fully fished	We buy Turtle-Safe® shrimp, certified by the Sea Turtle Restoration Project. Sea turtles can escape from the nets that catch these shrimp. However, bycatch of other animals (fish and invertebrates) is still high.
	Snow Crab	Bering Sea, Alaska	Fully fished	In response to a sudden decline in snow crab stocks, fishery quotas for 2000 have been slashed to less than 15% of the 1999 quotas. Managers predict that the fishery will be closed completely in 2001, and that these emergency measures will help the snow crab population recover quickly.
	Spot Prawns	West Coast N. America	Fully fished to **overfished**	In Monterey Bay, spot prawns are caught in both traps and trawls. Local fishers have kept the trap fishery sustainable for generations. But most spot prawns are now caught with trawl nets. The trawl fishery is still poorly regulated and there are concerns about overfishing. We recommend trap-caught spot prawns only.
	Yellowfin/Ahi Tuna	Pacific, Atlantic, Indian Oceans	Fully fished	Yellowfin populations are healthy. The yellowfin we buy is caught on longlines near Hawaii. In this area, longlines take very little bycatch. In other areas, longlines kill tons of unwanted fish, seabirds and other wildlife. This is one example of why we look closely at the source when we make our seafood choices.

Seafood Item	Where's it from?	Level of Fishing	More Information
AVOID			We avoid these species. Their survival is threatened by too much fishing, or they are caught or farmed in ways that damage the environment. Some of these fisheries are under new management plans to help them recover. When we see progress, we hope to buy them again.
Bluefin Tuna	Atlantic Ocean	**Overfished to depleted**	Due to poor management, the Atlantic bluefin catch is only 10% of what it was a decade ago. International management efforts have so far failed to recover this species. Quotas for U.S. fishermen are very small.
Bluefin Tuna	Pacific Ocean	Fully fished	Pacific bluefin are in less trouble than Atlantic bluefin, but management lags and fishing pressure is increasing.
Chilean Seabass/ Patagonian Toothfish	Fleets from many countries fish in Patagonian and Antarctic waters.	**Overfished**	Heavy, unregulated fishing is wiping out this slow-growing, deep-ocean species. In 1998, the illegal catch was ten times the legal catch.
Cod, Atlantic	North Atlantic	**Overfished to depleted**	Cod's firm white flesh made it a favorite for fish and chips. But loose management, overfishing and destruction of undersea habitat have pushed this fish past its limit. Managers are working to help cod populations recover, but meanwhile cod needs a break.
Lingcod	West Coast N. America	Fully fished to **overfished**	Lingcod are alarmingly overfished. New restrictions are in place to help this species recover.
Monkfish	New England and mid-Atlantic	**Overfished to depleted**	Monkfish, caught in the same nets as Atlantic cod, became popular as the cod got scarce. Now monkfish too are overfished.

Orange Roughy	New Zealand	**Overfished to depleted**	This deepwater fish was heavily fished until the population crashed. Orange roughy grow slowly—market-sized fish can be 50 to 80 years old. New management, with strict quotas, is now in place.
Rockfish (also called Pacific Red Snapper or Rock Cod)	Alaska, Washington, Oregon, California	Fully fished to **overfished**	There are more than 60 species of rockfish along the U.S. West Coast. Rockfish reproduce slowly, so they can't take heavy levels of fishing. We're no longer serving rockfish in our restaurant. In the California-Oregon-Washington fisheries, rockfish species threatened by overfishing include bank rockfish, darkblotched rockfish, silvergrey rockfish, Pacific Ocean perch, bocaccio and canary rockfish. Quotas for many species have been slashed. New management plans are being developed to protect overfished species and to manage bycatch. Off Alaska, the status of most rockfish populations is unknown. Because different species of rockfish share the same habitat, they are often caught together in one net. It's difficult to avoid catching overfished rockfishes while trawling for more plentiful species.
Sablefish (Black Cod, Butterfish)	West Coast N. America	Fully fished to **overfished**	Sablefish populations have been in decline since 1980.
Salmon	Pacific Northwest, Chile, Great Britain	Farmed	We don't buy farmed salmon. Raising salmon in ocean pens pollutes the water with feces and can spread disease to wild salmon. Farmed salmon eat fishmeal made from ocean fish, so salmon farming hurts ocean food chains. Also, it's usually Atlantic salmon that are farmed—even in the Pacific. Salmon that escape from farms can cause problems for native wild salmon.
Sea Scallops	East Coast N. America	**Overfished**	Sea scallops are overfished in New England. We're monitoring efforts to help sea scallop populations recover.
Shark (all)	Worldwide mainly tropical countries	**Overfished**	Sharks reproduce slowly. They can't withstand heavy fishing, and most species are overfished. Many sharks are killed just for their fins, used in shark-fin soup. Millions of sharks also die as wasted catch in nets and on longlines meant for other kinds of fish.
Shrimp/Prawns	Various –	Farmed	Some shrimp farms were built by destroying mangrove forests and other coastal habitat, where wild shrimp and fish feed and breed. We're looking into shrimp that is farmed inland using environmentally-friendly methods. We'll switch to farmed shrimp when we find a sustainable source.
Swordfish	Pacific, Atlantic, Indian Oceans	Atlantic **overfished to depleted,** Indian Ocean uncertain, Pacific fully fished	In the Atlantic, many years of fishing have greatly impacted the swordfish population. Today, the average swordfish caught in the north Atlantic weighs just 90 pounds, compared to over 200 pounds in the 1960s. These small swordfish are caught before they have a chance to reproduce, so the population is in a downward spiral. A new international agreement to reduce the catch of swordfish has been adopted, and the U.S. National Marine Fisheries Service has implemented new protection for juveniles. We're monitoring these new efforts to let populations recover. While Pacific swordfish are not in such serious trouble, we're concerned about bycatch in this fishery.

COASTAL ZONE MANAGEMENT

© Bret Forb

It's clear that poor management or misguided land-use practices cause many of the problems faced by both fresh and salt water ecosystems. This is why it's important to manage the entire coastal zone — which encompasses both the water and the watershed — rather than just shorelines or bodies of water. Many countries now recognize that this approach to coastal protection is necessary and are taking steps toward more complete coastal zone management.

One example is the 1972 United States Coastal Zone Management Act (CZMA). Through economic incentives the CZMA encourages (but does not require) individual coastal states to take a strong role in protecting their coastal zone. The act also attempts to enhance commitment and consistency among all coastal states in the way they manage their resources.

Another significant piece of legislation that protects and sustains US coastal resources is the 1972 Marine Protection Research and Sanctuaries Act. The act permits the federal government to designate specific areas for research, protection and recreational purposes using a philosophy of *multiple compatible use*. This philosophy recognizes that coastal resources have numerous shareholders, and all must have a voice and take responsibility for protecting the coastal zone.

On a local level, you can help by supporting legislation that implements responsible coastal zone development strategies and integrates decision-making across jurisdictions and ecosystems.

Although sometimes it might seem like one small voice will not be able to do any good, this is not the case. There are numerous examples where grass-roots efforts and responsible development have been able to create an environmentally friendly solution to an impending problem. For example, the Mitsubishi corporation was involved with the Mexican government and the salt production company Exportadora de Sal S.A. de C.V. (ESSA) to expand their salt production facilities in Baja, Mexico to the San Ignacio Lagoon, one of the last calfing grounds for the grey whale. In the ensuing political discussion, after scientific review and Environmental Impact Assessment, the consortium decided not to build the proposed saltworks based upon several reasons, one being the overwhelming negative reaction by environmental organizations such as Project AWARE Foundation. Another example, further into Mexico, sea turtles are facing problems from development but the efforts of citizens and environmental organizations have slowed development. X'cacel Beach in Quintana Roo, Mexico is a 2.6 kilometre/1.6 mile-long stretch of beach along the Cancun-Tulum tourist corridor. This is the principle nesting site for Loggerhead and Atlantic Green Sea Turtles on the Atlantic coast. In 1998, part of this area was sold to the Sol Melia hotel chain so they could develop a 450 room complex. This development threatens to destroy the beach as nesting habitat for the sea turtles. The involvement of the public through petitions, demonstrations and the efforts of numerous environmental organizations such as Greenpeace, The World Conservation Union (IUCN) and Project AWARE Foundation have all contributed to the slowing of this development. As of this writing the conflict over the development of the land was in the hands of the Mexican government.

Counter to the trend in development, public involvement in marine protected areas can contribute to the sustainable use of the aquatic environment. A prime example of this is the Blongko Marine Sanctuary in Minahasa, North Sulawesi, Indonesia. Originally supported by USAID and Proyek Pesisir (the Indonesian Coastal Resources Management Project), the sanctuary was formed by local Blonko villagers after they saw a similar measure at nearby Apo Island. The Blongko villagers formed a community driven sanctuary. This community sanctuary effort makes the resource users into resource managers and helps them have an active role in resource sustainablility. The Blongko Marine Sanctuary is an effective model for this type of grass-roots effort that can lead to widespread habitat protection.

Another way to show your support of coastal zone management is by practicing sustainable eco-tourism. You can stay at resorts that center their business around ecologically friendly operations. A prime example is the Maho Bay group of lodgings. Located on Saint Thomas in the United States Virgin Islands, Maho Bay consists of four separate resorts. The group of lodgings coordinates recycling and reclamation of glass, aluminum, packing materials, paper, rainwater and wastewater. They maintain an organic orchard and garden using compost plus make use of alternative energy. The buildings on the property were constructed using "green" building materials with every precaution taken to minimize the effect on the environment. The Maho Bay resorts pride themselves on being good environmental neighbors on the island by incorporating sound environmental practices into their business operations. This type of sustainable eco-tourism is gaining in popularity. As more patrons choose these environmentally friendly alternatives the aquatic world can only benefit.

INTERNATIONAL MEASURES

Beyond UN fisheries legislation and national coastal zone projects, a concerted international effort to protect and conserve the world's ocean has been taking place for many years. Here's an historical look at some of the more significant measures:

1972 – London Convention on the Prevention of Water Pollution by Dumping of Wastes and Other Matter (also called the Ocean Dumping Convention). Prohibited marine dumping of persistent plastic material.

1973 – London International Convention for the Prevention of Pollution from Ships (also called the

> THE DISCHARGE OF PLASTIC OR GARBAGE MIXED WITH PLASTIC INTO ANY WATERS IS PROHIBITED. THE DISCHARGE OF ALL GARBAGE IS PROHIBITED IN THE NAVIGABLE WATERS OF THE UNITED STATES AND, IN ALL OTHER WATERS, WITHIN THREE NAUTICAL MILES OF THE NEAREST LAND.
>
> | THE DISCHARGE OF DUNNAGE, LINING, AND PACKING MATERIALS THAT FLOAT IS PROHIBITED WITHIN 25 NAUTICAL MILES FROM THE NEAREST LAND. | OTHER UNGROUND GARBAGE MAY BE DISCHARGED BEYOND 12 NAUTICAL MILES FROM THE NEAREST LAND. | OTHER GARBAGE GROUND TO LESS THAN ONE INCH MAY BE DISCHARGED BEYOND THREE NAUTICAL MILES OF THE NEAREST LAND. |
> |---|---|---|
>
> A PERSON WHO VIOLATES THE ABOVE REQUIREMENTS IS LIABLE FOR A CIVIL PENALTY OF UP TO $25,000, A FINE OF UP TO $50,000, AND IMPRISONMENT FOR UP TO FIVE YEARS FOR EACH VIOLATION. REGIONAL, STATE, AND LOCAL RESTRICTIONS ON GARBAGE DISCHARGES ALSO MAY APPLY.

Placard Required by MARPOL Annex V of all US Vessels at least Eight Metres/26 Feet in Length

Marine Pollution Convention). Established regulations controlling oil pollution and the disposal of packaged substances, sewage and garbage. In 1983 an addition to the London Convention placed a moratorium on the dumping of low-level radioactive waste.

1973 – International Convention for the Prevention of Pollution (MARPOL). Regulated waste discharge — oil, noxious liquid substances, harmful substances, sewage and garbage — from ships.

1980 – the United Nations Environment Program (UNEP), the International Union for the Conservation of Nature and Natural Resources (IUCN), also known as the World Conservation Union, and the World Wildlife Fund (WWF) produced a document called the World Conservation Strategy. The document is an action plan representing the combined efforts of more than 700 scientists to devise a worldwide resource management strategy. It includes procedures for nations to develop their economic potential without destroying resources.

1991 — The Madrid Protocol on Environmental Protection to the Antarctic Treaty provided for the comprehensive protection of the Antarctic environment, and set firm standards governing human activities there. It banned mining and oil exploration in the Antarctic region for a minimum of fifty years and designated the entire continent, and its dependent marine ecosystem, as a "natural reserve devoted to peace and science."

Much has and is being done in the international arena to protect the world's oceans, but there is still a long way to go and difficult decisions to be made.

© NOAA/Department of Commerce

WORKING TOGETHER

In 1974, the World Conservation Strategy established a Regional Seas Programme to encourage countries sharing a common sea to find regional solutions to marine problems. Nations bordering marine regions work together to form action plans specific to the environmental needs of the area. Regional Seas Programmes have been established in 13 regions with 140 participating countries.

These include:
- Black Sea
- Caribbean
- East Asian Seas
- Eastern African
- Kuwait
- Mediterranean (the Blue Plan)
- North West Pacific
- Red Sea and Gulf of Aden
- South Asian Seas
- South East Pacific
- South Pacific
- South West Atlantic
- West and Central Africa

QUIZ

1. What steps do environmental organizations believe must be taken to conserve the world's fisheries? (choose all that apply)
   a. Establish and enforce international minimum fish conservation and management standards.
   b. Require alternatives to destructive fishing gear.
   c. Reduce existing economic incentives for unsustainable fishing.
   d. Protect and restore important marine habitats.
   e. Reduce bycatch.
2. Effective coastal zone management encompasses the following:
   a. water and watershed management.
   b. shoreline management.
   c. body of water management.
   d. all of the above.
3. The International Convention for the Prevention of Marine Pollution (MARPOL) regulated which of the following waste discharges from ships? (choose all that apply)
   a. oil.
   b. noxious liquid substances.
   c. harmful substances.
   d. sewage and garbage.

How did you do? 1. a, b, c, d, and e ; 2. d; 3. a, b, c, d

CHAPTER EIGHT
WHAT YOU CAN DO TO PROTECT THE AQUATIC ENVIRONMENT

DIVING AWARE

WHAT YOU CAN DO TO PROTECT THE AQUATIC ENVIRONMENT

- **DIVING AWARE**
- **GETTING INVOLVED**
- **REMOVING DEBRIS FROM THE AQUATIC ENVIRONMENT**
- **MOORING BUOYS**
- **MARINE PROTECTED AREAS**
- **ARTIFICIAL REEFS**
- **THE FUTURE**

STUDY QUESTIONS
Underline/highlight the answers to these questions as you read:
1. How can you be an environmentally friendly diver or snorkeler?
2. What environmental causes can you become involved in?
3. How can you responsibly remove trash from aquatic environments?
4. What is a mooring buoy and how does it protect the aquatic environment?
5. How can divers and snorkelers support protected areas?
6. What advantages do artificial reefs provide to nearby natural reefs?

The first step to AWARE diving is to change your attitude to that of a guest, not a consumer. Guests adjust their behavior to accommodate their host; customers do not. Guests respect and defer to their host and the local culture while customers demand service and accommodation. With this change in attitude will come a change in your interactions with the aquatic environment.

Behaving as a guest often means taking a passive rather than active role when interacting with aquatic life. However, passivity is rewarded – you're likely to see natural animal behavior. Think about this the next time you eagerly swim after a grouper or school of spadefish. Customers are those who treat the underwater world like an amusement park but guests approach their dive as they would a hike through an undisturbed forest.

Furthermore, AWARE divers recognize the most rewarding experiences are those in which the environment is altered as little as possible, such as fishwatching or responsible underwater photography. AWARE divers appreciate the full diversity of aquatic habitats. These include some areas that many divers never consider, such as grass beds, mangroves and even rubble zones. Armed with a little knowledge, you'll soon appreciate how important and interesting these often overlooked environments really are.

Also, consider your dive technique. AWARE divers leave the environment the way they found it, or even a little better.

© Michel Verdure

The key is excellent buoyancy control—the most important skill for any AWARE diver. It allows you to stay off the bottom while diving and avoid accidental contact with sensitive aquatic life. To fine tune your buoyancy if you haven't been diving for a while, you acquire new gear or you simply want to brush up, consider enrolling in the PADI Peak Performance Buoyancy Specialty course.

Another technique for AWARE diving is to act like a fish. Streamline yourself to avoid dragging equipment and damaging the environment (as well as your gear). Use clips, cords and holders to keep all accessories, gauges and alternate air sources close to your body. And when you move, swim slowly and methodically to avoid disturbing aquatic life. You can also use environmentally-friendly propulsion and avoid pulling yourself along the bottom — even incidental contact can be harmful to aquatic life. Be conscious of the location of your fin tips while kicking or hovering. Since fin damage is one of the biggest causes of unintended damage to environments such as coral reefs, position your legs higher than your head and hands to avoid touching the reef or the bottom.

AWARE diving doesn't necessarily mean that you can't collect game. Underwater hunters have long been some of the most ardent conservationists. But any ethical underwater hunter knows that there must be responsible limits and a willingness to abide by appropriate laws and regulations. If you *do* choose to take game, follow the appropriate laws or regulations and only take what you will personally consume. It's not necessary to take your legal limit just because you can.

If you take underwater photographs, be particularly aware of your movements. Before you take a camera underwater, consider your buoyancy skills. Watch where you put your hands, feet, fins and camera when setting up shots. In some locations, underwater photography has a bad reputation because of the irresponsible actions of a few photographers. Don't be one of them.

When people realize the ramifications of dying oceans and waterways in peril and take action, miracles are possible. Don't just dive, dive AWARE.

Learning to Scuba Dive—Becoming an Ambassador for the Aquatic Realm

It's difficult for anyone who regularly puts on a mask, or spends a lot of time in and around the water, not to notice adverse changes to the aquatic environment. In fact, because of their up-close-and-personal relationship with the underwater world, divers and snorkelers are often the first to recognize habitat decline and sound the alarm. This reinforces divers' natural roles as ambassadors for the protection and conservation of aquatic resources.

Divers are also the first to witness improvements when corrective steps begin to solve problems. As aquatic ambassadors, divers, snorkelers and other water enthusiasts carry the responsibility to share these environmental successes.

GETTING INVOLVED

Divers are generally a deeply committed and highly active community, particularly involved in protecting the aquatic environment. Some common diver activities include cleanup campaigns, monitoring and supporting marine protected areas and various conservation-oriented legislative efforts.

Today, the millions of recreational divers and tens of millions of snorkelers represent a powerful political constituency. An organized effort can influence environmental policy. Such a large aquatic constituency offers much-needed support for the creation of protected areas, strong and effective water quality regulations, and legislation protecting endangered and threatened marine species. This is where Project AWARE Foundation comes in. As the leading nonprofit organization in the dive community dedicated to preserving the aquatic environment, they organize major environmental protection initiatives (such as "Save the Sharks" campaign and "Protect the Living Reef" campaign) and local-based programs (such as International Cleanup Day). Your support for these activities and this organization can translate into real action to protect the resources which mean so much to us all.

REMOVING DEBRIS FROM THE AQUATIC ENVIRONMENT

In 1986, the Center for Marine Conservation launched what has become one of the largest of all community-based environmental events—International Cleanup Day. For several years this highly publicized event has increased public awareness and encouraged people to clear debris and trash from their local beaches. In 1995, this effort expanded from beaches to the entire aquatic world with the cooperative efforts of PADI and Project AWARE Foundation.

This once land-based event has grown to incorporate the underwater world as well. Each third Saturday in September, divers, snorkelers and local beachgoers congregate to clean up local beaches and waterways above and below the surface. This annual event mobilizes tens of thousands of divers around the world who participate — not only to help in the effort, but also to document the variety of trash they've amassed.

You can contact Project AWARE Foundation for more information about International Cleanup Day. You'll receive a booklet containing detailed guidelines about conducting an underwater cleanup, including data report forms from the Center for Marine Conservation.

> **EQUIPPING YOURSELF FOR TRASH**
> Before you head out to clean your dive site, make sure that you have properly equipped yourself with:
> 1. Exposure suit, including gloves to protect yourself
> 2. Short-nose clippers or stainless steel safety-end scissors to cut monofilament fishing line, if necessary
> 3. A small mesh bag to hold trash
> 4. A small flashlight underwater to check for living organisms inside any trash collected

But you don't have to wait for International Cleanup Day to begin removing debris from your aquatic environment. Imagine making dives all over the world and not seeing trash underwater. If the majority of recreational divers that entered the water removed one or two pieces of trash, the aquatic realm, down to 60 metres/130 feet, would be a lot cleaner than it is today. The most popular dive sites would be practically spotless — no cans, bottles, plasticware or fishing line. On a grand scale, divers everywhere would have a massive positive effect on the condition of the aquatic realm.

Regardless of the type of dive you're doing, chances are you have the time to pick up a few pieces of trash. Picking up underwater trash can become a second objective of every dive. Yet, even with the best of intentions, you might not be ready to remove trash—at least not without causing more harm to the environment. Appropriate removal of underwater rubbish often means more than just picking something off the bottom. You must first make sure that removing the item won't cause damage. This often requires a few inexpensive accessories which you can add to your predive equipment checklist.

If you find a heavy piece of pipe, anchor or some other unwieldy item, you'll need to use a lift bag to remove the debris. Make sure that you have the appropriate training and never use your BCD as a lifting device. If you accidentally released the object, you might ascend at an unsafe rate.

When you find trash underwater, you have an important decision to make - to remove it or leave it. Generally, you want to remove trash that is free from growth or is not a home for aquatic life. For example, if a can is only covered with ubiquitous algae and nothing is living inside it, you probably want to remove it. On the other hand, if a bottle is encrusted with large corals and has a few shrimp inside, you probably want to leave it underwater. Inspect your collected trash on the bottom. If you find fish, crustacea or other active creatures making the debris home, make an attempt to gently remove them near the bottom so the organism can quickly find a hiding place. If you can't remove the animals without harm, leave the object underwater. Also, if anything looks remotely suspicious — leave it alone. For example, if you find an unmarked 108 litre/55 gallon drum, firearms or ammunition, set a marker buoy to indicate its position for later collection by authorities.

Once back on board the boat or on shore, examine each piece of trash one more time. If you find animals are hiding in the trash, place the entire object in a bucket of water. If animals leave the object, throw the trash away and return the animal to the water close to where it was found, if possible. If the animals inside the trash don't leave, return the trash to the bottom. If you discover a suspicious or potentially hazardous object after your dive, transport it carefully or turn it over to local authorities. Also, recycle what trash you can — it doesn't help much to simply move trash from the bottom of the ocean to a landfill.

Rubbish removal is, unfortunately, only temporary but data collection is the first step to a permanent solution. Keep track of where and what kind of trash you find and send itemized lists to the Center for Marine Conservation.

By properly picking up underwater trash, you can make the aquatic realm much cleaner than it is today. The phrase *each one remove one* symbolizes the commitment to this effort.

FISHING LINE

On most dives, in just about any environment, you can find monofilament fishing line. Its presence underwater is hazardous for divers and aquatic creatures. When removing fishing line:

1. Work in two-person teams. One diver coils line as the other untangles it. Each person in the team should remain in each other's view.
2. Swim along the line, coiling it loosely around a dowel, small block or gloved hand. Collecting fishing line without coiling it can leave you or your buddy vulnerable to entanglement.
3. Use short-nosed clippers or scissors to cut line. Fishing line is frequently embedded in, or tightly wrapped around coral, sea fans, sponges or other aquatic life. Pulling it out might damage the reef unnecessarily but clippers and scissors allow for precise and safe removal of line.
4. Watch for fishhooks. Embed any you find in a piece of wood block, dowel or place them in a small container. If hooks cannot be transported safely, leave them underwater.

The fishing manufacturer Pure Fishing has set up monofilament recycling bins in local tackle stores. In the United States, to find a tackle store recycle bin near you, call (877) 777-3850, Ext. 8419.

STOPPING TRASH AT THE SOURCE

Although efforts to clean beaches and waterways are a step in the right direction, this does not address the fundamental cause of the problem. As divers and water lovers we are the first to see the negative effects of pollution, dumping and marine debris, but where does this problem originate?

There are two major categories of pollutants, point source and nonpoint source. Point source pollution comes from pollutants that originate from a known single point of discharge conveyance, such as a discharge pipe from a sewage treatment plant. Nonpoint source pollution is pollution that enters water from dispersed and uncontrolled sources, such as surface runoff, rather than through a pipe from a particular location. Nonpoint sources like forest and agricultural practices, on-site sewage disposal, storm drain runoff and recreational boats, may contribute pathogens, suspended solids and toxins to the water. The cumulative impact of nonpoint source pollution is significant.

What can you do to help? Control of point source pollution is best left to governmental agencies. But you can help the problem of nonpoint source pollution. Simply, you can curtail your contribution to nonpoint source pollution at home. Many problems can be traced upstream in a watershed to residential users. Users upstream, in non-coastal areas are often unaware of the consequences of the actions they take for the water downstream. Here are some simple suggestions that you can follow to make your local, or not so local waters beautiful.

- Make people aware. Most people do not purposely and knowingly try to pollute the environment, they simply do not realize what they are doing is detrimental. As a diver, you know what can be harmful. Make sure others understand the actions they take at home can have harmful consequences for the ocean and waterways downstream.
- Keep your residence clean. Sweep your sidewalks, dispose of trash, toxins and other dangerous chemicals properly, *not* in the stormdrain. Stormdrains flow directly to waterways, *not* into treatment facilities.
- Plant instead of paving. Increasing permeable cover such as plants, grass and shrubs not only makes your residence more attractive, it minimizes the runoff from your property.
- Reduce your pesticide use. Residential pesticide users often apply and misapply much more chemical than is necessary. Read the label carefully and follow directions for disposal.
- Use nontoxic alternatives. Natural or less harmful alternatives exist for almost every type of cleaner, and pest control agent.
- Change your oil and discard used oil properly. Used motor oil is extremely toxic to the environment and collection points are often easily accessible. Dumping oil down stormdrains results in direct toxic contaimation of aquatic environments.
- Dispose of toxins responsibly. Never pour household toxins or cleaners down the drain, down a storm gutter or in a toilet. All toxic materials have guidelines for proper disposal. Contact your local municipality to find a hazardous material drop off point.
- Reduce, Reuse and Recycle. If you use less, you have less to worry about disposing of. Reduce by choosing items that have less packaging. Reuse by donating what you can to charity. Recycle by using or establishing a convenient recycling system in your area.

It might seem like a big job, but it's worth it. By making small changes in your residential practices, and advocating these changes to others, you will help create a stewardship for the environment that will translate into cleaner and healthier water.

MOORING BUOYS

In regions with delicate and vulnerable sea bottoms, such as coral reefs, one of the best ways to protect the aquatic environment is to avoid boat anchor damage. This can be done by either live boating (drift diving) or through installing permanent mooring buoys.

The mooring buoy concept is simple: install a mooring buoy close to or over a site where boats traditionally anchor. Instead of anchoring, boat users tie off to the mooring, lessening any potential damage. Moorings may be used to zone an area for a particular activity and help avoid conflicts between, for example, fishermen and divers. If an area is being overused, moorings can easily be removed, placed elsewhere, and replaced at the original site when it has had adequate recovery time.

Installing mooring buoys requires professional expertise at all phases of project planning and implementation. Several factors must be considered, including the scope of the project, the anticipated use of the project site, the number, location and type of moorings deployed, funding for installation and ongoing maintenance and continuing educational programs.

Despite the effort involved in a mooring buoy planning and installation project, the benefits far outweigh the work involved. Mooring buoy projects are firmly fixed as a healthy addition to the future of the world's aquatic environment.

To learn more about mooring buoys, and about ways you can start your own program, a complete booklet – *The Mooring Buoy Planning Guide* – is available from Project AWARE Foundation. A copy of this guide can also be downloaded from www.projectaware.org.

A Diver Installing a Mooring Buoy to Protect a Reef From Anchor Damage

MARINE PROTECTED AREAS

One of the best ways to conserve the aquatic environment is to create protected areas. Parks, reserves and sanctuaries have all demonstrated, in varying degrees, that protection results in aquatic life population recovery. Anecdotal perception and scientific study supports this idea in the Florida Keys National Marine Sanctuary, in Florida, USA, where fish populations began a strong recovery just one year after the implementation of no-take zones.

But financial support and strong management plans are required so that protected areas are more than conservation areas in name only. Some marine protected areas raise funds to implement and enforce the management plans by charging users fee — so please keep this in mind the next time you dive in a protected area. Some locations, such as the Bonaire Marine Park, transformed their annual users pass into a collectable token. The public support for the park has resulted in several requests by mail from divers who are eager to purchase the current year's edition.

But you can do much more than just pay fees or make donations. Most protected areas have volunteer programs allowing you to get involved, such as assisting with mooring installations, monitoring activities or interpretation, such as campfire talks. Contact your local park or sanctuary manager for details. Also, don't forget that management plans depend upon public participation. Use your influence as a diver and a resource user to ensure protected areas remain protected.

SCIENTIFIC OR CONSERVATION ORGANIZATIONS USING VOLUNTEERS

If you want to get involved and use your knowledge and skills, consider volunteering for environmental activities or programs in your area. The following organizations depend upon volunteers to make their valuable work possible and meaningful.

The Artificial Reef Society of British Columbia (ARSBC)
Phone: 604-733-1217
E-mail: publicrelations@artificialreef.bc.ca
www.artificialreef.bc.ca

Australian Marine Conservation Society (AMCS)
Phone: +61 (0)7 3848 5235
Email: amcs@amcs.org.au
www.amcs.org.au

Center for Marine Conservation (CMC)
Phone: (202) 429-5609
Email: cmc@dccmc.org
www.cmc-ocean.org

The Coral Reef Alliance (Coral)
Phone: (510) 848-0110
Email: info@coral.org
www.coral.org

Marine Conservation Society (MCS)
Phone: 01989 566017
Email: info@mcsuk.org
www.mcsuk.org

Oceanwatch Foundation
Phone: (954) 467-1366
Email: info@oceanwatch.org
www.oceanwatch.org

Project AWARE Foundation
Phone: (949) 858-7234, ext. 439
Email: aware@padi.com
www.projectaware.org

The Reef Environmental Education Foundation (REEF)
Phone: (305) 451-0312
Email: reef@reef.org
www.reef.org

ReefKeeper International
Phone: (305) 358-4600
E-Mail: ReefKeeper@ReefKeeper.org
www.reefkeeper.org

The Shark Trust
Phone: +44 (0)1752 672008
Email: sharkwebmaster@pro-enterprise.co.uk
www.sharktrust.org

United Nations Environment Program - World Conservation Monitoring Centre (UNEP-WCMC)
Phone: +44 (0)1223 277314
Email: info@unep-wcmc.org
www.unep-wcmc.org

ARTIFICIAL REEFS

Artificial reefs provide structure and relief in areas that are otherwise devoid of bottom features. In addition, they also provide the hard substrate necessary to sustain invertebrate life such as mussels, sponges, scallops and sea fans. In featureless sand flats, this additional structure increases the available habitat for these animals. Since these organisms are often the support for higher levels of the food web, an increase in invertebrate numbers leads to greater populations of both resident fish and transient fish populations such as sharks, jacks and tuna.

Of course, people can also benefit. Artificial reefs not only enhance fishery resources but also dive opportunities. For example, the Texas, USA artificial reef program has led hundreds of thousands of divers offshore each year. Just the same, artificial reefs can give natural reefs a much-needed break by reducing diving and fishing pressures. The theory is simple:

The more people who use artificial reefs, the fewer use natural ones. Natural reefs therefore have time to recover and replenish.

Artificial reefs also offer excellent opportunities to learn more about the local environment because many jurisdictions require monitoring of artificial reef areas. In these cases, volunteer research programs gather scientific data. An example of this is the Artificial Reef Society of British Columbia (ARSBC), located in Vancouver, British Columbia, Canada. A volunteer organization, the ARSBC is dedicated to enhancing the marine environment and sport diving through the creation and preservation of artificial reefs. In the past six years, the ARSBC has sunk five decommissioned military ships as artificial reefs and has used volunteers to prepare the ships for environmentally sound placement, as well as establishing marine life monitoring programs after sinking.

Project AWARE Foundation Grant Program

Effective conservation measures require funding. Recognizing this reality, in 1992, Project AWARE Foundation established a Grant Program to support education, research and public service projects regarding the aquatic environment. The Grant Program has spread to many Project AWARE Offices around the world.

The Foundation's Grant Program operates on a calendar year funding cycle and supports worthwhile aquatic conservation projects. The Micro Grant Program provides funding for local grass roots efforts, including projects such as local beach cleanups, mooring buoy programs, local education programs and research projects. The Macro Grant Program provides funding for regional, national or international efforts, including projects such as public awareness campaigns, broad-based education programs, citizen outreach programs, and high profile or large scale events.

The Project AWARE Foundation devotes nearly 50 percent of its expenses to the environmental grant program. It is from the funding awarded through this program that hundreds of important conservation projects and studies have occurred. The more support we receive from our patrons and donors, the more environmental projects will be funded through this program.

© R.E.E.F.

Project AWARE Foundation (Americas)
30151 Tomas Street
Rancho Santa Margarita, CA 92688
Phone: (949) 858-7234 or (949) 729-7237, ext. 659
Fax: (949) 858-7521
Email: aware@padi.com

Project AWARE (Asia Pacific)
Unit 3, 4 Skyline Place
Frenchs Forest
New South Wales 2086
Sydney, Australia
Phone: 61 2 9451 2300
Fax: 61 2 9451 9999
Email: neilg@padi.com.au

Project AWARE (United Kingdom)
Unit 7, St. Philips Central
St. Philips, Bristol BS2 0P0
Great Britain
Phone: 44 117 300 7234
Fax: 44 117 971 0400
Email: suzannep@padi.co.uk

Project AWARE (Europe)
Oberwilerstrasse 3 CH
8442 Hettlingen, Switzerland
Phone: 41 52 304 1414
Fax: 41 52 304 1499
Email: aware@padi.ch

Projects Funded by Project AWARE Foundation Grant Program

THE FUTURE

What does the future hold for the aquatic environment? The answer is up to us. Throughout this text, you have read about numerous problems plaguing our water planet, from simple lack of knowledge and understanding, to careless human actions and wasteful destruction. You've also read about many giant strides that have been taken to provide further protection for our aquatic environment, from legislative initiatives to public education. So we must realize that these are times of change and it is our responsibility to influence what direction change will lead us next.

The aquatic environment, for example, has endured many changes over the years. It's seen global warming and warmer sea temperatures, coastal development and coastal zone destruction, overfishing and species depletion. Some experts claim the health of our aquatic environment is spiraling downward. Others point to positive trends, such as increased public awareness and community action, to refute that belief.

It's no secret that our aquatic environment is in trouble and needs our help. We have polluted our oceans, lakes, rivers and waterways. We have overfished food fish to the point of depletion. We have altered coastal zones and wetland areas with increased development. And although we have caused so much devastation to the aquatic environment, we also nurture it back to health.

In the late 1960's and early 1970's, we began to see the aquatic environment as a fragile ecosystem requiring care instead of an infinite resource able to withstand mankind's

pressure. The "out of sight, out of mind" philosophy of using oceans, lakes, rivers and waterways as dumping sites for garbage and waste started to change. We began to open our eyes to the problems we caused. Public awareness about the condition of our aquatic environment began to rise.

People concerned about the aquatic environment banded together to form environmental groups and organizations. Some groups campaigned publicly while others worked with lawmakers. Several important laws setting precedence for the protection of endangered species, preservation of clean ocean water and management of sustainable fisheries was passed during this period. Since then, many of these same environmental groups have grown into highly effective nonprofit organizations representing large constituencies who work regularly with government agencies to reauthorize and strengthen current conservation laws, initiate environmental activities and educate the public.

Attitudes and behaviors have changed over time. We are now focusing on things we can do to preserve our precious resources; communities are working together to clean up the aquatic environment and volunteerism is on the rise. Project AWARE Foundation is optimistic as we head into the future because of increased numbers of participation in activities such as International Cleanup Day, Dive Into Earth Day, diver monitoring programs, the advancement of environmental research and the attention paid to environmental legislation.

Simply by reading this book, you are one of the many who are interested in preserving our aquatic environment. Through cooperative action, raising the collective consciousness and making our voices heard, we can influence the future of our aquatic environment.

QUIZ

1. To dive aware, you should: (choose all that apply)
   a. Interact passively with the environment.
   b. Perfect your buoyancy control.
   c. Streamline your dive equipment.
   d. Collect a shell to remember your dive.
2. True or False. Divers are a large and powerful political constituency who can effect environmental policy.
3. You can responsibly remove trash from the aquatic environment by taking which of the following actions? (choose all that apply)
   a. Participating in International Cleanup Day.
   b. Picking up all debris, even if it has animals in it or on it.
   c. Removing trash or debris on every dive.
   d. Collecting data on trash you remove from the aquatic environment.
4. True or False. Mooring buoys protect the aquatic environment from anchor damage.
5. Divers and snorkelers can support aquatic protected areas by taking which of the following actions? (choose all that apply)
   a. Making a donation to the protected area.
   b. Participating in any of the protected area's volunteer activities.
   c. Discouraging the use of protected areas so they remain unused.
   d. Participate in any public meetings regarding the protected area.
6. Artificial reefs benefit natural reefs by: (choose all that apply)
   a. Providing additional hard substrate.
   b. Reducing diving and fishing pressure on the natural reef.
   c. Gathering scientific data on reef development.
   d. Enhancing fishery resources.

How did you do? 1. a, b and c; 2. True; 3. a, c and d; 4. True; 5. a, b and d; 6. a, b, c and d.

GLOSSARY

aerobic – occuring only in the presence of oxygen.

algae – ancient group of primitive plants that support major marine food webs.

anaerobic – occuring only in the absence of oxygen.

Antarctic Bottom Water – large volume of cold, dense and saline water that forms in the Weddell Sea and moves north from the Antarctic continent.

aphotic zone (also profundal zone) – the dark zone past which any light penetrates the water

aplacental viviparity – method of reproduction where eggs develop internally without a connection to the uterus.

aquaculture – growing or farming of plants and animals under controlled conditions in an aquatic environment.

artificial reef - placement of a suitable, long-lived, stable and environmentally friendly material such as steel or concrete on a particular area of seafloor. This increases the amount of hard substrate necessary for reef formation.

asexual – reproduction of an organism without formation of a zygote.

benthic zone – the zone of the ocean floor.

bilge – the lowest point of a ship's inner hull. A bilge pump is used to remove water that collects there.

bioaccumulation – concentration of a pollutant as it makes its way up the food chain and is concentrated.

biocide – substance that is harmful to many different organisms.

bioluminescence – Production of nonthermal light by living organisms.

biotic reef – reef that is caused by or produced by living things.

bivalve – class of mollusca that includes clams, oysters, mussles and scallops.

blade – algal equivalent of a leaf.

brine – seawater or saltwater.

bycatch – fishing catch that is unintended and incidental to the primary target species.

byssal threads – produced by bivalves to attach the organism to the substrate.

calving – process of forming icebergs where large blocks of a glacier are undercut and fall into the ocean.

Challenger Deep – the deepest part of the ocean's deepest trench, the Marianas Trench. It is 10,870 metres/35,640 feet deep.

coastal zone – the zone from the ocean to as far inland as the environment is immediately affected by marine processes.

continental rise – the portion of a continent that extends from a steep cliff that falls off to the ocean floor.

continental shelf – the submerged and gradually sloping part of a continent.

continental slope – the sloping transition between a continent and the seabed.

coral – cnidarians of the class Anthozoa that can generate hard calcareous skeletons.

coral bleaching – sometimes reversible disease in which corals expel their brown-colored zooxanthelle and turn white. It is thought that this is linked to global warming.

coral reef – linear mass of calcium carbonate assembled from coral and related organisms.

cultural eutrophication - rapid addition of nutrients to a freshwater body from sewage and industrial wastes.

dichloro-diphenyl-trichloroethane (DDT) – chlorinated hydrocarbon insecticide banned in the United States for its damaging effects to invertebrates.

de jure praedae – one chapter of the 1604 Hutgo Grotius work that formed the basis for modern international oceanic law.

deep ocean – the portion of the ocean where there is little additional change in density with increasing depth and home to more than 80 percent of the ocean's total water volume.

deforestation – the clearing of forests.

desalinization – the process of removing salt from seawater or brackish water.

desiccation – drying.

detritus – finely divided remains of plants, animals or both.

dinoflagellate – planktonic single-celled flagellate responsible for red tides.

ecosystem – a community and its environment that functions as an ecological unit.

ecotourism – tourism that is often to undeveloped areas, preserves nature, is ecologically sustainable, contributes to the preservation and conservation of the area and has minimal effects on the site.

eelgrass – group of marine angiosperms found in protected regions gloabally.

Exclusive Economic Zone (EEZ) – the offshore zone past 370 kilometres/200 miles from a contiguous shoreline.

El Nino – southward flowing nutrient-poor current off of South America's west coast.

endemic – native to a particular region or area.

epifauna – animals that live on the ocean bottom.

epiphytic – living on the surface of plants.

estuary – body of water partially surrounded by land where fresh water mixes with sea water.

eutrophication – physical, chemical and biological changes resulting from excessive nutrients introduced into water.

finning – process of removing the fins from a shark for commercial use and discarding the remainder of the animal.

fishery – combination of fishers and fish in a region, usually grouped by target species or equipment used.

food web – group of organisms linked through feeding relationships.

freshwater – water with low to no salt.

gestation – the time between fertilization and birth.

global commons – oceans that lie outside national borders.

gradient – a change in a quantity with a change in a variable.

gross primary production – total production from photosynthesis without adjustment for respiration.

groundwater – water that is in the ground and supplies wells and springs.

halocline – ocean zone where salinity increases rapidly with depth.

halogenated hydrocarbon – halogen derivative of organic hydrogen and carbon containing compounds. Hydrocarbons contribute to air pollution problems such as smog.

hermatypic – coral species possessing symbiotic zooxanthellae and producing calcium carbonate reef structure.

holdfast – branching structure that anchors algae to the substrate.

hydrocarbon – organic compound containing carbon and hydrogen. Common in petroleum and natural gas.

hydrosphere – the area that includes all water on the planet and in the atmosphere.

hydrothermal vents – spring of hot mineral and gas rich seawater found on some oceanic bottoms.

infauna – benthic organisms that live wholly within the substrate.

inorganic material – any matter other than plant or animal.

intersitial fauna – animals that live between sediment particles.

intertidal zone – part of the seashore exposed during low tide but underwater at high tide.

International Union for the Conservation of Nature and Natural Resources (IUCN) – Also called The World Conservation Union, has a membership of 181 countries and aims to influence, encourage and assist societies throughout the world to conserve the integrity and diversity of nature.

kelp – the group of large brown algae of the orders Laminariales and Fucales.

kelp forest – groupings of brown seaweeds such as *Macrocystis* that support a diverse range of plant and animal species.

keystone species – an organism whose effect on the ecosystem is greatly disproportionate to its abundance.

krill – small, shrimp-like crustacean, *Euphausia superba* that is common in Antarctic water.

larva – pre-adult stage of organism that does not resemble the adult.

Law of the Sea – 1982 draft convention adopted by the United Nations that defines regulations on territorial waters, exclusive economic zones, the high seas and other provisions.

lentic – still waters, such as ponds, lakes and swamps.

limnetic zone – zone of open water in a freshwater body of water.

limnology – study of freshwater.

littoral zone – the intertidal zone

live rock - described as a single living marine organism or an assemblage of marine organisms, attached to a hard substrate such as a rock. It is used primarily in home reef aquariums.

London Dumping Convention – officially titled the Convention on the Prevention of Marine Pollution by Dumping of Wastes and Other Matter, this 1972 convention regulates ocean dumping as defined as deliberate disposal at sea not related to the normal operation of vessels.

long-line – commercial fishing method involving a long section of floating line with vertical section extending down, at the end of which is a baited hook.

lotic – actively moving water such as a river.

manganese nodules – nodules found on the ocean floor comprised primarily of manganese.

mangrove – tropical plant that grows in salt marshes and tidal estuaries.

mantle – layer of earth between above the core but below the crust.

mare liberum – reprint of one chapter of Hugo Grotius' 1604 work, *De Jure Praedae*, which formed the basis for modern international sea law.

Marianas Trench – deep ocean trench near the Marianas Islands with a recorded depth of 11,708 metres/38,635 feet.

MARPOL – The 1973 International Convention for the Prevention of Pollution From Ships. This agreement's intent is to end the deliberate, negligent or accidental release of harmful substances from ships.

marsh – brackish water area next to salt water.

mid ocean ridge – connected series of undersea mountains.

mooring buoy - permanent buoy designed for short time anchorage that employs an embedment type anchor. It is used by boaters to secure their boat without risking damage to the bottom.

multiple compatible use - philosophy promoted by the 1972 US Marine Protection Research and Sanctuaries Act, which recognizes that the numerous shareholders of coastal resources must all have a voice and take responsibility for protecting the coastal zone.

munitions – ammunition.

neritic zone – zone of nearshore water over the continental shelf.

nonpoint source pollution – pollution that enters the water from many sources rather than one specific site. Examples include urban runoff and agricultural activities.

nutrient – chemical substance neccesary for life in the sea, excluding carbon dioxide, oxygen and water.

organic material – derived from living matter.

overfishing – harvest of fish that exceeds the ability of a species to reproduce.

overgrazing – animal grazing to the point of damage to vegetation. Also a source of increased runoff.

overturn – mixing of layers in standing water.

oviparous – method of reproduction where eggs are produced that hatch outside the body.

ozone – molecule with three oxygen atoms that forms a protective layer in the upper atmosphere protecting organisms from dangerous solar radiation.

oviparous – reproductive method where eggs are produced that hatch outside the mother's body.

PADI – Professional Association of Diving Instructors.

PADI Dive Center or Resort – dive facility meeting and maintaining a high level of service, equipment, training and safety as specified by PADI standards. PADI Dive Centers typically cater to local clientele while PADI Resorts normally service dive travelers.

Polychlorinated biphenyls (PCBs) – chemical once commonly used in cooling appliances and potentially responsible for harmful effects on marine mammals.

petrochemical – chemical derived from petroleum or natural gas.

plankton bloom – sudden and dramatic increase in the number of phytoplankton often linked to an increase in available nutrients.

photic zone – zone to which depth light penetrates the water column – rarely deeper than 200 metres/660 feet.

photosynthesis – conversion of light energy into chemical energy using chlorophyll. This process consumes carbon dioxide and water and produces glucose and oxygen.

phyla – one of the major groups of the animal kingdom.

phytoplankton – plant plankton.

pinniped – suborder of the order Carnivoa that includes sea lions, seals and walrus.

placental viviparity – method of reproduction where the organism develops a yolksac placenta from which the embryo receives nutrients.

polynya – gap in the polar ice pack where liquid water and the atmosphere meet.

pneumatocyst – gas-filled air bladder in algae that supports the plant and lift it to the surface of the water.

point source pollution – pollution resulting from direct dicharge, such as a pipe, into water.

predation – one organism consuming another.

productivity (also primary productivity) – production of organic material from inorganic material through photosynthesis or chemosynthesis.

profundal zone – see aphotic zone.

Project AWARE (Aquatic World Awareness, Responsibility and Education) – PADI's environmental awareness and protection philosophy. Through their training, PADI Divers learn the importance of protecting fragile aquatic ecosystems and are encouraged to become involved in preservation efforts.

Project AWARE Foundation – dive industry's leading non-profit, tax-exempt organization committed to the conservation and preservation of the aquatic environment and its resources.

pyncocline – zone where seawater density increases dramatically with depth.

radioactivity – spontaneous decay of an element's isotope.

red tide – phytoplankton bloom, usually dinoflagellate, resulting in rust-colored water.

salinity – amount of dissolved inorganic minerals (salt) in seawater, usually measured in parts per thousand or grams per kilogram of water.

seagrass – marine angiosperms that are not seaweeds, such as *Zostera*.

seining – fishing method using a net that hangs in the water with one edge held by floats and the other on the bottom. Bringing the two edges of the net together then catches fish.

sessile – attached to the bottom and unable to move.

shelf break – junction of the continental slope and shelf where the slope dramatically increases.

spoil – byproduct of dredging operations.

sporophyte – diploid (having the basic number of chromosomes doubled) stage of a plant's life cycle.

stipe – marine algae's equivalent to terrestrial plant's stem.

stormdrain - urban drain that collects water which flows untreated directly to a lake, river or other waterway.

substrate – solid surface where an organism lives or is attached.

supralittoral – also called the splash zone, this intertidal region is from the highest reach of spray to mean high tide.

thermal stratification – formation of different temperature layers in water.

thermocline – area in water in which temperature changes most rapidly with increasing depth.

tidal flat – flat coastal area consisting of mostly loose sediment that is inundated periodically by tidal action.

tragedy of the commons – title from 1968 work of Garrett Hardin in which some populations had agricultural holdings where the benefit was kept by one but the cost was distributed to all. Applies to fisheries in that the benefit of catching fish (profit) is kept by a few, but the cost (declining fish stocks) is borne by all.

trawling – fishing method where resources are collected from the sea floor by a net dragged over it.

upwelling – circulation of deep nutrient-rich water moving towards the ocean surface.

wetland – land where water dominates type of plants and animals that live there.

zonation – bands of distinct species groups that develop in the intertidal.

zooplankton – animal plankton.

zooxanthellae – photosynthetic plankton (usually dinoflagellates) that live symbiotically within the tissues of some invertebrates, most noticeably coral.

zygote – cell formed by the joining of two gametes.

REFERENCES

Beatley, T., Brower, D. & Schwab, A. An Introduction to Coastal Zone Management. Washington, DC: Island Press.

Charton, B. (1988). The Facts on File Dictionary of Marine Science. New York, NY. Facts on File Inc.

Covering the Coasts: A Reporter's Guide to Coastal and Marine Resources. Washington, DC. National Safety Council Environmental Health Center.

Davidson, O.G. (1998). The Enchanted Braid: Coming to Terms With Nature on the Coral Reef. New York: John Wiley & Sons, Inc.

Earle, S.A. (1995). Sea Change: A Message of the Oceans. New York: Fawcett Columbine/Ballantine Books.

Garrison, T. (1999). Oceanography: An Invitation to Marine Science (3rd edition). New York: Wadsworth Publishing Company.

The Handy Science Answer Book. (1994). Detroit, MI. Visible Ink Press.

Hinrichsen, D. (1998). Coastal Waters of the World: Trends, Threats and Strategies. Washington, DC: Island Press.

Lalli, C & Parsons, T. (1993). Biological Oceanography: An Introduction. Oxford: Butterworth Heinemann.

Lerman, M. (1986). Marine Biology: Environment, Diversity and Ecology. Menlo Park, CA: The Benjamin/Cummings Publishing Company.

Levinton, J. (1995). Marine Biology: Function, Biodiversity, Ecology. New York, NY: Oxford University Press.

Norse, E.A. (ed.). (1993). Global Marine Biological Diversity. Washington, DC: Island Press.

Pernetta, J. (ed.) (1994). Philip's Atlas of the Oceans. London: George Philip Ltd.

Pickard, G. & Emery, W. (1990) Descriptive Physical Oceanography: An Introduction. Oxford: Butterworth Heinemann.

Ricketts, E., Calvin, J & Hedgpeth, J. (1985). Between Pacific Tides. Stanford, CA: Stanford University Press.

Safina, C. (1992). A Primer on Conserving Marine Resources. Islip, NY: National Audubon Society Living Oceans Program.

Safina, C. (1997). Song for a Blue Ocean. New York: Henry Holt and Company.

Seeds, M. (2000). Horizons: Exploring the Universe. Pacific Grove, CA: Brooks/Cole.

Valiela, I. (1995). Marine Ecological Processes. New York: Springer.

Viders, H. (1995). Marine Conservation for the 21st Century. Flagstaff, AZ: Best Publishing Company.

Waller, G. (ed.) (1996). Sealife: A Complete Guide to the Marine Environment. Washington, DC: Smithsonian Institution Press.

Wells, S. & Hanna, N. (1992). The Greenpeace Book of Coral Reefs. New York: Sterling Publishing Co.

INDEX

A

adaptation, intertidal plants 41
aerobic 21
agricultural runoff 116
agricultural waste 75
algae 43, 49
alien species 88-90
Amoco Cadiz 110-111
anaerobic 21
anchor damage 76
anoxic 112
Antarctic Bottom Water 56
Antarctic Circumpolar Current 28
Antarctic Treaty, the 57-58
Antarctic, resources 57
Antarctica, continent 56-57
aphotic zone 25
aquaculture 100
Arctic Ocean, the 58
Arctic, resources 59
Artificial Reef Society of British Columbia (ARSBC) 145
artificial reefs 10, 144-145
AWARE Fish Identification Specialty course 68, 71

B

ballast water 88-89
Baltic Sea, The 111-113
benthic zone 21
bioaccumulation 83
bioluminescence 29
biotic reef 62
Blongko Marine Sanctuary 129
bottom dredge 96
bottom trawl 96
bycatch 95-96, 98
bykill 96
byssal thread 41

C

Caribbean Sea, The 115-117
Center for Marine Conservation 86, 138, 139
Challenger Deep 18
chemical pollutants 83-85, 113
Chlorofluorocarbons (CFCs) 56
coastal development 148
coastal zone management 31, 128-129
coastal zone, the 31-35, 101-103
community, kelp forest 51
continental margin 25
continental rise 25
continental shelf 25, 40
continental slope 25
coral bleaching 73
coral composition 63
coral, growth rate 65
coral, hermatypic 64
coral, location of 63
Coriolis effect 27, 28
cultural eutrophication 22
currents 28

D

De Jure Praedae 92
deep ocean 30
deep seabed 25
deforestation 75, 116
desalinization 113
detritus 21, 24, 34
dichloro-diphenyl-trichloroethane (DDT) 83, 113
Dive Into Earth Day 10, 149
diving AWARE 134-135
dredge spoil 86
driftnet 96

E

eco-tourism 129
eelgrass 43
El Nino 27, 73
epifauna 43-44
epiphytic algae 51
estuary 34
eutrophication 85, 112-113
exclusive economic zone (EEZ) 92
Exxon Valdez 82, 111

F

fertilizer 75
fin damage 135
fisheries 33, 91-100, 108
fisheries, as employment 92
fisheries, as food source 91-92
fisheries, collapse 94-95
fisheries, government subsidies 94
fisheries, responsible management 121-129
fisheries, worldwide 30, 91
fishery resources 144
fishery, shark 97-100
fishing line collection 139
fishing pressure 144
fishing regulations 123
fishing, explosives 75, 97
fishing, most productive areas 30
fishing, poison 75, 97
fishing, types of 96-97
food web 26, 144
fossil fuel 55
freshwater ecosystems 21-24
freshwater resources 102, 113

G

gametes 50
gestation, shark 98
giant kelp (Macrocystis) 50
gillnet 96
global commons 91
global warming 148
greenhouse effect, the 55, 76

gross primary production (GPP) 71
groundwater 102
Gulf Stream 28
gyre 28

H

habitat destruction 121
habitat restoration 121
habitat, coral 65
halocline 112
halogenated hydrocarbon 113
heat pollution 88
holdfast 41
human-induced threats,
    coastal zone 31-32
human-induced threats, coral 75-76
hydrilla 90
hydrocarbon 81, 83
hydrologic cycle, the 17
hydrosphere 16
hydrothermal vents 25

I

industrial waste 75, 108-109
infauna 43-44
integrated coastal zone management 31
International Cleanup
    Day 10, 137, 138, 149
international conservation
    efforts 130-131
interstitial community 44
intertidal zone 41-48

J-K

Jaws 99
juvenile organisms 44
kelp forests 49-53
kelp, distribution 49
kelp, human use 51
keystone species 48, 52
krill (Euphausia superba) 57

L

land-based waste 81, 101, 110
Law of the Sea, The 92
lentic ecosystems 21-22
life cycle, kelp 50
limnetic zone 21
limnology 21
littoral zone 21
live rock 75
London Dumping Convention 84-85
longline 96
lotic ecosystems 21, 22-24

M

mangrove 33-34, 103
Mare Liberum 92
Marianas Trench 18
marine nurseries 44
marine productivity 26-30
marine protected areas 142
MARPOL 130
marsh 35
Mauna Kea 18
Mediterranean, The 107-109
mid-ocean ridge 18, 19
mooring buoy 10, 76, 141
Mooring Buoy Planning Guide 141
Mount Everest 18
multiple compatible use 128
munitions 87-88

N

natural processes, coastal zone 31
natural threats, coral 73-75
Nature Conservancy, The 71
neap tide 42
neritic zone 25, 40
nonpoint source pollution 140
North Sea, The 110-111
Northern Polar Ocean, The 58-59
nutrients 26, 39

O

oil cleanup 82
oil disposal 140
oil drilling platform 81, 111
oil pollution 81-83, 109-110,
    110-111, 113, 117
oil pollution, consequences 82-83
oil pollution, vehicles 82
oil tanker accident 81
oil use 140
organic waste 85-86
Outer Continental Shelf Lands Act 92
overfishing 75, 94, 111, 121, 148
overgrazing 75
overturn 23
ozone layer 56, 76

P

PADI 7, 8, 68, 138
pair trawling 96
passive interaction 134
PEMSEA 31
Persian Gulf, The 113-115
pesticide 75, 116, 140
photic zone 25, 39, 40
photosynthesis 39, 50, 64
phytoplankton 21, 26, 29, 39, 115
plankton 29
plankton bloom 40
plastic 86-87
pneumatocysts 49
point source pollution 140
polar regions 54-59
polar zone, location 38
pollution 73, 80-90
polychlorinated biphenyls
    (PCBs) 83-84, 113
predation, rocky intertidal 47-48
primary productivity 39, 115
primary productivity, arctic 59
primary productivity, Arctic Ocean 54

primary productivity, polar 54-55
primary productivity, rocky intertidal 46
primary productivity, temperate seas 39
productivity, coastal waters 40
productivity, ocean 39-40
profundal zone 21
Project AWARE 8, 12, 76
Project AWARE Coral Reef
    Conservation Initiative 77
Project AWARE Foundation 9, 68, 129,
    137, 138, 141, 149
Project AWARE Foundation
    Grant Program 146-147
Project AWARE Protect the
    Living Reef campaign 137
Project AWARE Protect the
    Sharks campaign 100, 137
Project AWARE Specialty course 7, 9

Q-R

radioactivity 84-85
rainforests of the oceans 62
red tide 29, 85
reef ecosystem 64
Reef Environmental Education
    Foundation (REEF) 68, 71
reef fish 66-71
REEF Fish Survey Project 71
reef sensitivity 72-73
Regional Seas Programme 131
rocky intertidal zone 45-48
runoff 116

S

sandy shore 44
scuba diving, learning 136
sea level rise 55, 56
sea otter 51-52
sea temperature 76, 148
sea urchin (Stronglyocentrotus) 52
seafood contamination 85-86, 108

seafood, responsible
    choices 123, 124-127
seagrasses 43
seawater, mineral composition of 25
seaweed, intertidal 43
sediment, community 43
seining 96
semidiurnal 42
sewage 75
shark 70, 97-100
shark finning 13
shark management plan 100
shark, reproductive strategy 97, 98
shelf break 25
solid waste 86
Southern Polar Ocean 55-58
storm runoff 73
stormdrain 82, 140
Strait of Malacca, The 109-110
stream 35
streamlining 135
sustainable fisheries 124
sustainable use 129

T

temperate zone, location 38
temperature, aquatic 18-19
temperature, of Earth 56
territorial sea 92
thermal stratification 23, 39
thermocline 23
tidal cycle 42
tidal level, rocky intertidal 45
tidal zone 41
tides 42
tourism 75-76, 117
toxic algae bloom 108, 112
toxic waste 83
Tragedy of the Commons, The 91
trash collection 138-139
Truman Proclamation 92

U-V

underwater hunting 135
underwater photography 135
upwelling 26, 27, 30
US Coastal Zone Management Act 128
volunteering 142, 143

W-X-Y

warfare 109, 115
water, properties of 17
watershed 31
wetland 33-35

Z

zebra mussel 89
zonation, biological factors 46
zonation, intertidal 43, 45, 46
zonation, upper range 46
zooplankton 26, 29
zooxanthellae 64
zygote 50

KNOWLEDGE REVIEW

1. List three goals of Project AWARE
   1. _____
   2. _____
   3. _____

2. What are the two primary freshwater ecosystems and what distinguishes them?

3. The ocean is made up of two zones — the _____ zone or the zone of perpetual darkness and the zone of light penetration, which is the _____ zone.

4. What is upwelling and why is it so important to productivity and fisheries?

5. Rocky intertidal zonation depends on what three factors?
   1. _____
   2. _____
   3. _____

6. Why are coral reefs important to the aquatic environment?

7. List four human-induced threats to the coral reef environment:
   1. _____
   2. _____
   3. _____
   4. _____

8. What are the main sources of pollution in the aquatic environment?

9. What are three reasons that worldwide fisheries are facing collapse?
   1. _____
   2. _____
   3. _____

10. How does the global population increase along coastal shores affect the aquatic environment?

11. What are the main problems faced by the world's most environmentally threatened regions?

12. What steps are environmental organizations recommending be taken to conserve the world's fisheries?

13. How can you dive AWARE?

14. What are three actions you can take to responsibly remove trash from the aquatic environment?
    1. _____
    2. _____
    3. _____

Please visit www.projectaware.org to check your answers.

Student Diver Statement:
Any questions I answered incorrectly or incompletely I've had explained to me, and I understand them.

Name _____ Date _____

Knowledge Reviews may not be reproduced in any form without the written permission of the publisher.